APOSTLE EXTRAORDINARY

By the same author

THE STRANGER OF GALILEE
(Meditations on the Life of Our Lord)

BENEATH THE CROSS OF JESUS
(Meditations on the Passion of Our Lord)

THE UPWARD CALLING
(Meditations on the Christian Life)

INTO THE SAME IMAGE

THEY TEACH US TO PRAY

PRAYER IS THE SECRET

THE BIBLICAL DOCTRINE OF INITIATION

Apostle Extraordinary

A Modern Portrait of St. Paul

by

REGINALD E. O. WHITE, M.A., B.D.

William B. Eerdmans Publishing Company
Grand Rapids, Michigan

Library of Congress Catalog Card Number 62-18955

Printed in the United States of America

Preface

A PORTRAIT may teach us much — of the person portrayed, of the time and the cause and the faith he represents. Sometimes, however, the portrait is glazed, and as we approach we see dimly superimposed upon the painted figure the reflected image of ourselves.

Such is the purpose of this study of the Apostle Extraordinary, greatest of Christians, profoundest of teachers, staunchest of friends, most intrepid of adventurers, most dauntless of sufferers, most winsome of saints, Paul of Tarsus, soldier and slave and lover of Jesus Christ our Lord.

Contents

Paul the Debtor

Hebrew Born of Hebrews

Under Obligation to the Greeks

What I Also Received

Who Loved Me

1 Hebrew Born of Hebrews

"HE IS ONE of the few men in ancient literature who is absolutely modern," said the large middle-aged man seated on the deck of a tramp steamer heading for Cyprus through a sultry afternoon. His occupation, and obsession, was orange-growing in Palestine; he confessed to having enjoyed the war, but since then he had been up against things in a foreign country, with few friends and nearly penniless. Yet he had once written a textbook on St. Paul, and memories lingered. "You would not be surprised to meet him in a wayside inn, drinking a little wine for his stomach's sake, and if you had to borrow a dollar I think you'd rather ask Paul than anyone else."

An unconventional testimony to a historic religious figure, but a telling one! And this testimony is curiously paralleled by another, from a mind of very different calibre among Paul's twentieth-century biographers: "There is about Paul the same modernness as about Augustine . . . While many figures of the past are unintelligible and incomprehensible, he is as human as if he had walked in upon us out of the street."

The truth is, an immensely attractive personality, passionate, eager, alive, adventurous, appealing, stands behind the theologian, the contentious debater, the involved, impetuous writer, the haloed saint, of Christian tradition. One authoritative analysis lists logic, love of truth, argument, courage and intuition, extreme swiftness of mind and quickness of temper, among the varied elements of which his nature was composed. But above all he possessed the fact-loving mind, the impatient practicality, the unblinking realism, that mark the modern mind. He would have been equally at home in the present century as in the first — and far more comfortable. Indeed, it is doubtful if in some things we have even yet caught up with him.

For all this, Paul yet belongs unquestionably to his own age. In a unique degree he mediates to later ages through his own mind and heart, his work and his writings, the spiritual treasures, Hebrew, Greek and Christian, that make the first century of our era the great watershed of western civilisation. Religiously, the greatest of these inherited treasures were enshrined in Paul's ancestral faith, the Judaism of the synagogue, of Pharisaism, of the Old Testament.

Known, disliked, and envied throughout the Roman world, Judaism – in words of C. H. Dodd – "combined the splendour of antiquity, the tenacity of a national faith, and the direct personal appeal of a religion of heart and life." In addition, every significant growing-point of Jewish thought pointed forward to a pattern of fulfilment into which the Christian gospel fitted perfectly, as Paul discovered. Though we emphasise, therefore, the attractive fascination of the apostle's complex personality, it is strictly unavoidable to begin to sketch his portrait with that in him which many find least agreeable, his personal debt to Jewry.

Hebrew

All the deepest assumptions of Christianity are Hebraic in origin. God is one, holy, Creator and King, the living God. Man reflects in his own nature the divine personality, and is the object of God's infinite compassion and unrelenting purpose to save. History is the movement of the race under the divine hand towards a divine end, and all human hope is focussed upon a divine Messiah and a spiritual commonwealth or kingdom that shall recapture the lost paradise of old. Religion is essentially a relationship, of the spirit of man with the living God, expressed from God's side in revelation and a covenant of mercy, and from man's side in obedience, worship, faith and love.

Such elementary but determinative ideas formed the basis of every young Jew's education. They were illumined by stories of Abraham and the Exodus, of kings, prophets, saints and resistance leaders. They were dramatised in the great festivals of Passover, Tabernacles, Pentecost, Purim – and Tarsus was near enough to Jerusalem for Paul sometimes to attend. They were codified in the Law, and in the Torah's innumerable minute elaborations of the rules of the good life. And all were doubly impressed upon an eager and gifted young mind by the piety and affection of a sound family life – Paul was the son of a Pharisee – and the rigorous discipline of synagogue and school. Paul found that little of essential Judaism had to be left behind when he accepted Jesus as Judaism's heir, fulfilment, and goal.

Paul received from Judaism, however, more than the premise and pattern of all his thinking. To the end of his life the Old Testament scriptures possessed for him unassailable authority. "It is written" clinches every argument and forecloses all discussion for Paul himself, and (he assumes) for all Jewish readers, though he is aware that Gentiles need other persuasions. That Israel had been entrusted with "the oracles of God" was the chief of her "advantages", and Paul illustrates, in his deep knowledge of its content and his love of its sacred phrases, just how precious to a Jewish heart the Old Testament could be.

Sometimes Rabbinic methods of allegorising mark the apostle's use of scripture: he can argue doctrine from an ambiguous collective noun, and spiritualise the water and the rock of the wilderness as Christian sacraments. Yet he never confuses the real issues of Old Testament revelation, or misses its inmost meaning. Certainly he came to read the Jewish scriptures with Christian eyes, but he was convinced that to do so "removed the veil" from the Law and from the reading heart, the mist of incomprehension that hid from unbelieving Israel the true meaning and message of her incomparable divine literature. To the end, the Jewish scriptures nourished the faith, buttressed the arguments, armed the contentions, furnished the synagogue sermons, informed the counsel and illumined the experience of the Christian apostle.

Pharisee

That Paul was a Jew of the Dispersion, his education proceeding in the atmosphere of a Gentile city, would intensify rather than dilute his Jewish pride and patriotism, while his father's example would still further direct his thoughts toward what he later called "the strictest party of our religion", the sect of the Pharisees. It would seem, indeed, that Paul stood closer than did some of his colleagues to the original intention and piety of this puritan group within Judaism.

For the Pharisee movement came into prominence to defend all that was distinctively Judaist against the inroads of Greek and Roman paganism, and it served the nation exceedingly well in the maintenance of religion, law and morality. That it had decayed, by the first century, into self-righteousness, hypocrisy, and an unsympathetic and mechanical legalism, is clear from the strictures of Jesus upon its less worthy representatives; but sincere and godly men remained within the movement – men like Nicodemus, and Gamaliel, and Paul. From Gamaliel his tutor, the grandson of Hillel (one of Judaism's greatest and more liberal teachers), Paul would certainly learn what was best and most positive in the Pharisaic emphasis.

Final studies at Jerusalem brought Paul within the University atmosphere and to sit at the feet of this Rabbi famed throughout Jewry and far beyond, for wisdom, scholarship and pious statesmanship. Even more, it brought him to live within sight of the national shrine, and within reach of innumerable memorials of the glorious and exciting days of Israel's past.

Paul's academic progress was exceptional: he "outstripped his fellow students", and gave himself with ardour and application to his chosen career of Rabbi, "being zealous for God" and "more exceedingly zealous for the traditions of my fathers". He was rewarded, (almost certainly – Acts 26:10), in comparative youth, with a place in the supreme religious and civil court of Jewry, the Sanhedrin. In the synagogues of the Mediterranean cities later on, such qualifications provided both opportunities and authority for teaching, until from the tenor of his message the local Jews discovered the transformation of his thought.

The zeal here twice referred to constitutes the third of Paul's special debts to Judaism, though it is one not often mentioned: a religious passion of rare intensity and force. To the Jew, religion was ever the first and final preoccupation of life, as never to Greek or Roman, and very rarely to the western mind. In Paul's case, patriotism, Pharisaism, and the energies of a strong emotional nature, apparently undiverted into more domestic channels, were yet further reinforced by personal ambition and pride of success; and all was nourished by a depth of religious conviction and a strength of moral feeling of which very few Gentiles were capable.

The fundamental, half-realised assumptions of a man's thinking, his home training, his constant reading, his formal education, his loyalties, career and temperament, make up a very large part of his matured personality; and in Paul's life all were shaped and enriched by Judaism. Even had this Jewish heritage been all that Paul received, it is plain that he was wondrously equipped to become one of the world's religious leaders.

Christian Jew

Nor was Paul unaware of the greatness of his heritage, though his gratitude was mingled with a sharply realistic insight into Judaism's weaknesses and failures. To the end he made no secret of his Jewish origin, and so far from apologising for it, he repeatedly insisted upon the great advantages the Jew possessed – "who are Israelites, whose is the adoption, and the glory, and the covenants, and the giving of the law, and the service of God, and the promises, whose are the fathers, and of whom is Christ . . ." He insisted, too, upon his own rightful inheritance of these advantages, having been "circumcised the eighth day, of the stock of Israel, of the tribe of Benjamin . . ." The Temple remained dear to him, even to his last visit to Jerusalem, and he purposefully planned, whenever possible, to be present for the festivals. It was his unsuccessful attempt to placate Jewish feeling, and to show that despite his lifelong defence of Gentile liberty of faith, he himself was not alienated from Jewish piety, which provided occasion for his arrest in Jerusalem and his subsequent long imprisonment.

In the same way, the ancient promises made to Israel could not, by such a heart, be lightly set aside, though here Christian universalism and Jewish expectations together produce a somewhat involved conviction. Paul's intense distress at Israel's rejection of her Christ led him to echo, with much of its original agony of spirit, the great prayer of Moses, offered when Israel fell into apostasy at the foot of Sinai: "Yet now, if Thou wilt, forgive their sin – and if not, blot me, I pray Thee, out of Thy book . . ."

But Paul could not believe that all the past, and all the covenanted promises, must fail. He acknowledged that there had never been more than a remnant of Israel faithful to the purpose of God; that God was not bound to Israel by any necessity, or claim; that the fault lay wholly with Israel, a disobedient and obstinate people. But even so, the divine intention cannot be finally frustrated, and in the end Israel will surely return and inherit the promises, through Christ. The effect of Israel's temporary rejection will in fact be the vast extension of her privileges and blessings to all believing Gentiles.

What moves our admiration here is the combination of profound religious confidence in the stedfastness of God's promises, with an open-eyed assessment of Israel's past and present unworthiness. Deeply as he loved his people, Paul was bitterly aware of the betrayal of her heritage and destiny. Of some Jews he could say terrible things. As it was their privilege that "to the Jew first" the gospel should be preached, so with equal emphasis he insists that "upon the Jew first" shall judgement also fall – "wrath, indignation, tribulation, and anguish".

He can analyse with devastating exactness the self-righteousness of the Jew, resting on the Law, knowing the divine will, approving the things that are excellent, instructed out of the Law, a guide of the blind, light to the benighted, corrector of the foolish, teacher of babes. And he can no less sharply accuse the Jew of blatant hypocrisy that glories in the Law while transgressing it, and boasts of the knowledge of God while it dishonours Him.

For Paul charges Jewry with having earned a just reputation for immorality, adultery, theft; and for irreligion, in that they despise their own Law and pillage others' temples. "So that through them the very name of God is blasphemed among the Gentiles." He was obviously keenly sensitive to the evil odour that attached to the name of Jew, and to the Jewish ghettos, in Alexandria, Corinth, Rome, and elsewhere: nor was Paul by any means alone in this. The Pharisees generally, the reforming sects of Essenes, of Qumran, of John the Baptist, and certain other first-century observers and writers shared Paul's disgust and confirm his judgements.

Behind this trenchant criticism there doubtless lay much of personal disillusionment with Judaism, and a deep sense of the tragedy involved in the Messiah's rejection by His own people. He felt, too, the irony of the consequence: that having hounded their Messiah to the cross, the Jews then found a crucified Messiah the fatal stumblingblock to faith. Jewish treatment of Paul, aggravated by their fury at having lost his promising leadership and witnessed his defection, also reacted upon Paul. He recalls with some bitterness that the Jews "killed both the Lord Jesus and the prophets, and drove us out, and displease God and oppose all men, by hindering us from speaking to the Gentiles that they may be saved; so as always to fill up the measure of their sins." That he could nevertheless retain his pride and hope in Israel confirms the suggestion of his calmer writing, that the deepest of all reasons for this castigation of his countrymen's failures was his abiding love for his race, and his tenacious, unshaken belief in their unparalleled opportunity and destiny.

Some generations are much more aware of what they have achieved than of what they inherited, forgetting that the heritage makes the achievement possible. A humble appreciation of historic continuity, and a grateful sense of what one owes to the great intellects and saintly example of bygone ages, become ever rarer ingredients even of Christian character. Not every man has the insight to distinguish in his inheritance what is vital and enduring, and what is already, or must soon be, outgrown. Few have the courage to break completely with family tradition, racial loyalties, and established personal interest and ambition, in obedience to conscience and new truth. And very few indeed have shown, together with such insight and courage, the humility to acknowledge their immeasurable debt, nevertheless, for all that they had received. Among these very few, Paul well deserves his honourable place.

In the most famous of all the parables, Jesus pilloried the respectable, law-abiding Jew, jealous of his special privilege in the Father's house, believing himself ever obedient to the Father's will, and entitled as of right to the whole of the Father's inheritance – self-righteously unconcerned about the fate of the erring and ill-deserving, and resentful of the welcome offered to such as were penitent and willing to return to the Father's side. Very beautifully, C. H. Dodd suggests that the epistles of Paul show us the elder brother broken down by the Father's love, and leaving home and its secure delights to go into far countries – Cyprus, Pisidia, Macedonia, Greece, Rome – to seek out those brothers who still lingered among the swine and the husks.

So perfectly had the "Hebrew born of Hebrews" understood the mind and heart of the Jewish Messiah, the universal Christ, the Friend and Saviour of the world.

2 *Under Obligation to the Greeks*

IT IS ARGUABLE that when Paul spoke of being under obligation to the Greeks and to non-Greeks ("barbarians"), he was thinking of his obligation towards Christ to gather the Gentiles also into the kingdom of God, and not of any personal indebtedness to the Gentile world and its culture. Even so, the word Paul chooses refers explicitly to an acknowledged debt, something owed for favour received, and there is no reason to doubt that Paul, though once a Pharisee and now a Christian, would frankly agree that he had benefited in some respects from pagan, as from Jewish, influences.

Certainly he was proud of his birthplace, beautifully situated at the foot of the Cilician hills, astride the Cydnus, "a cool and headlong stream", and his phrase for Tarsus – "no mean city" – is not so much defensive as challenging. For Tarsus was no provincial backwater. "Highways of sea and land combined to make it one of the most important meeting-places of east and west", and the great trade routes which converged at the Cilician Gates kept it in touch with the world. Extensive trade brought to Tarsus the agents, and the produce, of a wide Mediterranean commerce, and its university brought, if not the numbers of visiting students that sought Athens or Alexandria, a fair proportion of them, and what is equally important, an influx of ideas. Its own students were respected far afield, even in Rome herself.

Honoured by both Mark Antony and Augustus, and accomplished in the peaceful arts of Roman city government, Tarsus developed an intense local pride, calling itself "Metropolis", "Temple-Keeper", "Free, First, Fairest and Best", in the fashion of a modern small-town publicity handout. Such feeling undoubtedly contributed to the young Paul's sense of citizenship and to his keen awareness of civic responsibilities. For beyond question Paul possessed later on a far more positive appreciation of the virtues of order, government, and social discipline than did many of his compatriots in that turbulent Jewish generation.

Moreover, even Paul's Jewish heritage was of that special quality which belonged to the Empire-wide Dispersion, with its Greek translation of the scriptures, its ubiquitous synagogues, its following of "God-fearers" (educated Gentiles attracted to but not finally committed to the Jewish faith), and its skilled apologists like Josephus and Philo presenting Jewish history and faith in their most favourable light to Gentile eyes — and in the process discovering an astonishing amount of Gentile thought within the Old Testament!

The more nationalistic and conservative Jews tended to exclude Gentiles from all interest in Messiah's kingdom, and the general separatist principles of Pharisaism certainly encouraged no compromise with paganism. On the other hand, the conversion of Gentiles could be regarded as the best proof of Jewish superiority, and of Messiah's victory; and there were Jews to whom the later Old Testament writings, as Ruth, Jonah, Zechariah, and parts of Isaiah, with their world-horizons, did not speak in vain.

The very existence of a Gentiles' translation of the Old Testament, the rite of proselyte baptism, and the number of "God-fearers" mentioned in the Acts of the Apostles, all illustrate Jesus' description of the Pharisees themselves as traversing sea and land to make one proselyte; while by the middle of the first century John the Baptist had ardent disciples as widely scattered as Alexandria, Ephesus, and probably Rome; and John had insisted that God could raise up children to Abraham wherever He chose. It is certain, therefore, that Paul was already confronted with "the Gentile question" long before his conversion.

Nor were these wider winds of Gentile influence confined to early days in Tarsus. Even in Jerusalem, in student years, impressions of pious patriotism and ancient glory were inextricably mingled with constant reminders of the presence of a Roman governor and an alien garrison, quartered almost within the Temple itself. When as a Christian Paul forcibly demands, "Is God the God of Jews only? Is He not the God of Gentiles also?" he is at once making articulate a fundamental question that had already vexed Judaism, and protesting its Christian answer.

We are not then surprised to find abundant evidence that, both directly and through Dispersion Judaism, the Graeco-Roman world had left its mark upon the ardent young Pharisee. With others of his kinsfolk, as Junias, Lucius, he bore from the first a Roman name, Paullus; yet others of the family, as Sosipater, Jason, Herodion, had Greek-sounding names. In later life he repeatedly claimed, and made the very most of, an inherited, though unexplained, Roman citizenship which conferred useful legal privileges.

It is especially revealing that Paul habitually quoted the Old Testament in its Greek version, which suggests that Greek was his mother-tongue and Hebrew only a second language. A few Greek quotation-tags — "In him we live and move and have our being" from Epimenides; "For we are indeed his offspring" from Aratus; "Bad company ruins good morals" from Meander; perhaps also "Cretans are always liars, evil beasts, lazy gluttons", also from Epimenides — may not indicate more than an alert mind in a Greek atmosphere, though they suggest more, just as Paul's express repudiation of "excellency of speech . . . of wisdom . . . enticing words" as weapons of the gospel reveals his knowledge of the characteristic traits of Greek rhetoric.

It is often emphasised that, in contrast to Jesus, Paul's is essentially a town-bred mind, and certainly the town's scenes and occupations linger in his speech, in metaphors of building, trade, slavery, of temples and citizenship, of buildings on fire, of soldiering, of the Tarsian Games — a very minor Olympic festival — in references to running, boxing, wrestling, and even metaphors of the pagan theatre-spectacles. But Paul's debt, and through him Christianity's debt, to that Graeco-Roman world must be measured by deeper things than names, and tricks of speech and style, or even civic or universalist impressions. The influences of that pagan society affected the embryonic apostle much more deeply than that.

Culture

Paul's inheritance of the Greek language gave him much more than "a sovereign command of the colloquial tongue of most of the known world", though that was indispensable equipment for a world missionary of the first century. It provided, in addition, ready to Paul's hand the most finely fashioned tool for his keenly analytic thought, penetrating enough to express his psychological insights, and flexible enough (at least under his inventive freedom to coin words and stretch syntax), to be adjusted to new uses and turned almost equally to argument, to eloquence, or to song.

Greek delight in philosophic discussion, alongside the widespread decay of faith in the old religious legends, created a popular audience for "lectures" and disputations such as Paul could conduct either on Mars' Hill at Athens or in the former School of Tyrannus at Ephesus. "Evangelists" of the Cynic or Stoic creeds were to be seen in every centre of population in the Near East, and they paved the way, and provided the pattern, for much propagandism in that enquiring and argumentative age. At Iconium, and on Mars' Hill, Paul demonstrated his sympathetic understanding of pagan thought no less skilfully than at Antioch in Pisidia he had shown his mastery of current Jewish questions.

The naturalistic basis of pagan religion, and the witness of creation to Something beyond itself, the law written on the heart even of the Gentile, and the preoccupation of the good pagan with questions of ethics, eschatology and judgement, Paul well understood. Both for his evangelistic approach, and for his illuminating criticism, Paul's insights into Graeco-Roman culture were invaluable to Christianity.

Similarly, it was clear gain for Christianity that her chief spokesman for the first twenty years of the new faith could mix familiarly with Roman officials, and claim the hearing, and the immunity, which Roman citizenship bestowed. No less important was the "imperialist" temper which grasped the immense strategic significance, for the gospel as for the Empire, of the great Roman roads and key cities. For Paul consistently planned his missionary journeys with something of the acumen and vision of a Roman military campaign, though health, circumstances, and persecution often interfered.

Paul's deepest response to the pagan culture of his time we have still to consider: but still speaking generally, Paul's relation to his Gentile environment is of the greatest importance if we are to understand the apostle himself. It is far too often assumed that for New Testament writers all divine revelation, and all divine mercy, were confined to Israel alone; that no gleam of truth or of the divine will was vouchsafed beyond the accepted confines of the Jewish-Christian movement.

The first chapter of John's Gospel might warn us to think more broadly of the life and light that were in the divine Word from the beginning, the life that was the light of men, – the true light that lightens every man, that was in the world even before the Word became flesh. God's approval of the pious heathen, Cornelius, and God's acceptance of his prayers, while he was not yet either within Israel or within the Church, should likewise prepare us for a wider view of the divine compassion.

But especially should Paul's insistence upon the revelation of God to the Gentiles through nature – "What can be known about God is plain to them, because God has shown it to them. Ever since the creation of the world his invisible nature, namely, his eternal power and deity, has been clearly perceived in the things that have been made. So they are without excuse . . ."; and his equal insistence that the Gentiles can "do by nature what the law requires", thereby showing "that what the law requires is written on their hearts", remind us that in Paul's thinking God is emphatically the God of the Gentiles also.

All truth, wherever it be found, is God's truth; all righteousness, all beauty, are of His inspiring. Christianity, as Paul taught it, is not the blunt negation of all other insights and ideals, but their fulfilment and perfection. God so loved the world –

Never was to chosen race
That unstinted tide confined;
Thine are every time and place . . .

and Paul knew that beneath all the error, falsehood, and sin of heathenism lay the truth suppressed by ungodly and wicked men. God had not left Himself without a witness: the earth was the Lord's, and Paul firmly believed that He would yet be called the God of the whole earth.

Rivals

That a mind so swift and alert, in an atmosphere so alive with controversy and stirred by powerful ideas, should reveal at many points the impression of its time, is scarcely surprising. But Paul also deliberately addressed himself so as to be heard and understood by his contemporaries. And he did this with such sympathy and skill and thoroughness as sometimes to be accused of borrowing where in fact he opposed, and of being indebted to ideas and beliefs which in truth he was striving to correct. Thus it is sometimes held that Paul learned deeply from Stoic philosophy, and borrowed formative elements of his gospel from the widespread Mystery cults. An impression is even given that Paul owed almost as much to his rivals as to his Lord!

J. S. Stewart has admirably summarised the resemblances between Paul and the Stoic teachers. As to style, Paul uses the imaginary dialogue, the rhetorical questions, the repartee, challenge, rejoinder, and irony, that were characteristic of Stoic debate. Some of his phrases, and some of his doxologies, are said to possess "the authentic Stoic ring". As to terms, Paul can use Stoic words like "conscience" – meaning an inner awareness of the moral law, imparted by nature; and "self-sufficiency" – meaning an inner independence of circumstance, of assistance, or of want (though Paul ascribes his "self-sufficiency" to the enabling of Christ). As to thought, Paul shares the Stoic criticism of society, the Stoic emphasis upon self-examination and prayer, its moral earnestness, and humanitarian spirit, its interest in "the deep things of the soul", its concern for moral reformation and rebirth.

Much of this sharing of ideas and expression was only to be expected. Tarsus was a centre of Stoic teaching, and had produced some world-famous leaders of the movement. More significantly, Paul was faced with essentially the same questions of psychology, of deliverance from sin and from death, of the decay of society and the dangers to social unity, that confronted Stoic thinkers also. And a man with Paul's passion to persuade could have no scruples about using the terminology, or the analysis, familiar to his audience in order to gain their attention, understanding, and assent.

But beyond that Paul does not go; his essential thought is very different from Stoicism. Stoic thought was pantheistic, owning no personal God. It offered no gospel to the fallen, the defeated, the afraid. It cultivated "apathy", the proud indifference of a perfectly disciplined soul: Epictetus could only bid a father kissing his child remember that it was a mortal thing he loved, and whisper while he kissed, "Tomorrow thou wilt die".

Such acceptance of fate, futility, and noble despair is very far from the prevailing spirit of the apostolic Church; while to say that Stoicism had no concept resembling even remotely Paul's doctrine of divine grace invading the sinful life to save, is to say that Paul and the Stoics dwelt in totally different intellectual and spiritual worlds.

As Paul could borrow and use with sovereign freedom the terms and concepts of Stoicism, where they suited, to express a far from Stoic philosophy and faith, so he could borrow and use, in the same freedom, some terms and notions in common use by the Mystery religions, while maintaining undiminished that independence of thought, and that hostility to all actual compromise with paganism, which was as much a part of Jewish as of Christian conviction. Whether Paul actually did so borrow and use such terms is less clear, for our knowledge of the Mystery cults of the first century is scanty.

The Mysteries used, at any rate in later times, terms like Lordship, salvation, eternal life, and practised rites of initiation and "communion" not unlike the Christian ordinances. The mystical cults, too, offered deliverance from all evil, in the world and beyond it, through participation in secret rites, and through mystical "union" with "divine beings", usually based upon possession of closely guarded secret "myths" concerning the dying and resurrection of the Mystery's god. In such "myths", the truth or otherwise of the story was irrelevant: knowing it, and participating dramatically in its meaning, saved the soul.

Paul, too, uses terms like Lordship, salvation, eternal life, communion, union with Christ, dying and rising with Christ, deliverance from sin and death; and he, too, can speak of the "mystery" hitherto hidden but now revealed by the divine Spirit. And he expounds Christian baptism as a being united with Christ in a death like His, so as to be united with Him in a resurrection like His – a dramatic participation in the passion of our Lord.

Yet here again, however closely Paul's language approximates to that familiar in the Mysteries, the essence of his thought is very far removed from the pagan myths. There is, surely, "all the difference in the world between a myth and a man", and Paul's whole message and faith began with the *historic* Jesus. Moreover, it was not knowledge, or rites, but faith which saved, in Paul's view: and that faith was focussed upon Christ, involving intellectual belief in the gospel story, self-renouncing trust in His redeeming power, personal adherence to Jesus as a living and personal Saviour and Lord, and ethical commitment to His standards as a pattern of daily life.

Central factors of Paul's message, history, gospel, faith, ethics, and moral purpose are not simply unparalleled in the Mystery Religions, but opposed to their whole outlook and method. There is a world-wide difference between moral salvation based upon what God has done within humanity, that sends one out to save humanity in God's name and love, and a "spiritual" or emotional ecstasy, called salvation, based upon possession of some secret knowledge, or performance of some secret rite, which has neither historical nor moral significance, and which one hugs proudly to oneself in isolation from the common, ignorant herd of ordinary men.

However persuasively Paul reworded his gospel in the thought-forms and terminology of his hearers, however he wrestled to make himself intelligible and his message acceptable, there remained no shadow of doubt in the mind of his audience as to what he meant. His gospel of the Crucified remained to the Greeks foolishness and, as at Athens, was greeted with derision. The persecution he faced, and accepted, in every Gentile city is the clearest testimony that in his presentation of the truth the offence of the cross was never evaded, nor the unique claim of Jesus to be the one Saviour of men, the life, the truth, and the only way, ever compromised or obscured.

Paul's attitude to these rival "faiths" effectively illustrates the true meaning of his oft-misquoted maxim: "I have become all things to all men, that I might by all means save some. I do it all for the sake of the gospel . . ." Too often this is interpreted in a morally slipshod, intellectually superficial, way, as excusing any abandonment of truth and principle in order not to offend – or still more often, in order to avoid discomfort for ourselves. For Paul it expressed the very reverse, a costly and demanding mental and spiritual effort of communication and reconciliation. "Live with your contemporaries", keeping in touch with your own generation and not with the one just behind you, is counsel easier to give than to follow, especially for those instinctively conservative minds inclined always to look back one stage for their inspiration and ideals. Yet we have, after all, to present Christ to our own time; and this means for us as for Paul, the ceaseless mental endeavour to translate the unchanging truth into the changing thought-forms and living terms of successive generations, without for a moment betraying the everlasting gospel, or compromising the essential and inescapable offence of the cross.

Paul was a man of his environment, complicated and many-sided as that was, as well as a man of God; and by great energy and flexibility of mind, and even greater human sympathy, he ministered with relevance and power to the generation to which he belonged, yet over against which he stood in Christ's name, beseeching reconciliation. That same Graeco-Roman world in which he found so much to criticise, so much to distress his Jewish-Christian soul, had yet helped to make him what he was. That is a part of the explanation of Paul, an important element in the providential preparation of the man for the task.

"How could it be, that the whole Church failed to grasp the universalist intention of Jesus, that men should come from north, south, east and west to sit with Abraham, Isaac and Jacob in the kingdom of God, and the gospel should be preached among all nations and to every creature, until Paul, who was not even one of the Twelve, showed them what He meant?"

The answer lies in the complex personality of the man God chose, and fashioned – a Hebrew born of Hebrews, yet a Jew of the Dispersion, a citizen of the Empire, surrounded and quickened by all the currents of thought in a university city on the frontier where Greece and Rome together touched the Orient, with a lively and sensitive natural sympathy with all sorts and conditions of men, and a consuming loyalty and love for Jesus, Messiah of the Jews, but Redeemer of all mankind.

3 *What I Also Received*

It was Paul's habit to dismiss distortions of his meaning with a vehement phrase which older versions translated as "God forbid!", and which newer ones, stifling its imprecatory overtones, render by numerous variations of "No! no!", "Far from it!", and "By no means!". One wonders with what vigorous language he would repudiate the nineteenth-century suggestion that he himself was the true founder of the Christian faith. One can imagine no "compliment" which would have distressed or angered him more, especially because of his intense love for Christ, but also because of his loyalty to those who, in his own words, "were in Christ before me".

Paul knew well his indebtedness to the Church of Christ, extending already, when he was converted, from Jerusalem and Samaria to Caesarea and Damascus; and what he knew he readily acknowledged. It is true that he claimed independent certainty concerning the message he preached, and independent authority for his apostolic office. But independence and gratitude are not incompatible in a character as rich as Paul's, and while for necessary purposes of controversy, or to protect from interference his infant Gentile Churches, he will assert emphatically his direct, unmediated, divine commission, he no less emphatically affirms his loyalty to the common faith, and his excellent terms of fellowship, without submission or tutelage on either side, with those who remained of the original apostles. This is his attitude in the letter to the Galatians.

Twice Paul explicitly refers to "what I also received". On one occasion he is referring to the account given of the origin of the Lord's Supper; and he insists, of course, that the ultimate source and authority for what he taught about it was the Lord Himself: "I received from the Lord what I also delivered to you . . ." But there is no reason whatever for supposing that he claims some wholly supernatural revelation about it made to himself alone, and the verbal resemblance between what he says and the Gospel accounts is so close as to leave no doubt that he received the story of that final scene in the Upper Room "from the Lord", but through the existing Church and its teaching.

It is highly significant that this central ordinance of Christian worship, recalling and proclaiming the Lord's death until He comes, was already a focal point of the Church life into which Paul came. And equally significant that in expounding baptism in his letters to two Churches he had not visited – Rome and Colosse – he could assume both the existence of the rite and a common tradition concerning its meaning. Between them, baptism and the Lord's Supper enshrine a great deal of the Christianity which Paul "received".

The second time Paul uses the phrase "what I also received" is in reference to a summary of the Church's faith in the resurrection of Christ, and the evidence therefor. It is a simple statement, and very ancient, as the use of the name Cephas for Peter sufficiently shows. This again Paul handed on, but as the common heritage of the Church's faith: "You received . . . what I also received . . . Whether then it was I or they, so we preach and so you believed." It seems likely, too, that the rhythmic and pithy summary of Christian insights concerning the divine and human person of Jesus which opens the epistle to the Romans is similarly a quotation from some early statement of the common faith.

From Jesus

Paul's admission of indebtedness goes further, however, than confessing his share in the worship and the faith which all Christians enjoyed. He frequently cites as his authority for counsel and judgement the clear and binding instructions of the Lord. Concerning clean and unclean meats he writes, "I know and am persuaded *by* the Lord Jesus that nothing is unclean in itself . . ." (where the rendering by the KJV has abundant support elsewhere in the New Testament, and implied anyhow in the modern translations "*in* the Lord Jesus". Only Jesus Himself could have persuaded a Pharisee on this point!).

Concerning marriage, Paul cites a "charge" given not by himself but by the Lord, prohibiting divorce; and he adds that concerning the unmarried he has "no command of the Lord, but I give my opinion as one who by the Lord's mercy is trustworthy". The great care with which Paul here distinguishes between the words of Jesus and his own counsel – "To the rest I say, not the Lord, that if . . ." – is striking evidence of the reverence with which he treated the sayings of Christ.

Concerning Christian organisation, "the Lord commanded that those who proclaim the gospel should get their living by the gospel." About the last things, Paul declares "by the word of the Lord" the certainty of resurrection and the equal participation of all who believe, in the final glory.

Beside these explicit appeals to treasured utterances of Jesus, there is on every page of Paul's letters evidence of close acquaintance with the teaching of the Master. One scholar estimated over a thousand parallels between words of Paul and words of Jesus, and though this is usually regarded as exaggerated, it is still impressive indication of the place Christ's pronouncements held in the thinking of the apostle.

Paul's advice about the Christian's relation to the State and to its officials echoes closely the dictum of Jesus about rendering to Caesar the things that are Caesar's. His appeal that Christians return good for evil, blessing for reviling, and his strictures upon the critical spirit, betray his knowledge of the Sermon on the Mount. Expressions like "remove mountains", "thief in the night", "Be careful for nothing", "blind leading the blind", "Jews require a sign", "Be vigilant . . . watchful", "all appearing before the judgment seat", "losing . . . gaining . . . what things were gain" and many others are all phrases which Paul, too, might put into quotation marks.

One saying of Jesus we owe entirely to Paul's memory, or at least to his record: "It is more blessed to give than to receive." Some think that in his words about mutual forgiveness, and in his use of "Abba-Father" as a kind of shorthand phrase for Christian prayer, Paul half-consciously quotes the Lord's Prayer.

Interesting though these half-echoes of the voice of Jesus are, still more important are those basic assumptions of Paul's thinking which are traceable directly to Jesus and to His story. Christ's incarnation "in the fulness of time"; His birth "of a woman", "under the law", "of the seed of David"; and the lowliness, the Servant-guise, of His human life, are silently assumed. The identification of Jesus with the Messiah of the prophecies, His "pleasing not Himself", His meekness and gentleness, His obedience and endurance,

Paul simply takes for granted as common Christian know-
edge. And so is the love regnant over all other qualities i
the character of Jesus, so eloquently described in Paul'
hymn to love.

Jesus' trial before Pontius Pilate, His crucifixion "i
weakness", His burial, and resurrection, His several Easte
appearances, and His "sending forth" of the Spirit, are al
presupposed in Paul's letters. Christ's ruling conception o
Christian life, as the life of sonship in the Father's family
was learned only at Christ's feet, as was the new meaning o
the kingdom of God. Beneath all Paul's theologising and
psychological analysis, the meaning of faith, and its primacy
in Christian experience, are the same for Paul as for Jesus.
And his attitude to the Jewish Law is also very similar: for
Paul, as for Jesus, the Law is divine, yet insufficient to
save, and all too often reduced to mere bondage.

As significant, for the Jewish mind and the trained Pharisee, is Paul's whole-hearted acceptance of the new principle, that love is at once the Law's supreme requirement, its fulfilment, and its end. For that is precisely what Jesus taught the zealous young scribe.

It is but just to conclude that Paul's dependence upon Jesus is everywhere manifest, and deliberately so. Our difficulty is that we assume this must have been so, and fail to appreciate with what diligence, thoroughness, and care, without a New Testament in his hands, Paul must have applied himself to "learning Christ". He had soaked his memory in the sayings and deeds of Jesus, he had adjusted his thought and his judgement, against all the pressure of his training, to the insights and principles of Jesus, and he had been changed, in outlook, ambition and spirit, into the likeness of Jesus. That is what is really meant when we say, somewhat too lightly, that Paul loved Christ.

Through the Church

But by the same token, Paul's debt to the earliest Christians is equally plain. It has been well said that "In none of the central affirmations of the Christian message can Paul be regarded as an innovator", and in everything, including his knowledge of Christ, Paul shared the faith and memories of many who followed Jesus before he did. We would give much to know whether he ever saw Christ. To

lentify Paul with the "rich young ruler" of the Gospels is
iere wishful thinking, but it is by no means improbable
iat Paul was in Jerusalem during Christ's ministry, and
is ambiguous phrase about knowing Christ "according to
esh" may just possibly hint at this. It could be that he
voids mentioning it more plainly because of painful re-
iembrance of his attitude at that time. We cannot know.

Paul's detailed appeal to the sayings of Jesus would not
i any case be likely to rest upon personal remembrance of
hrist's oral teaching, but upon a memorised (or written)
adition of His sayings which we are fairly sure circulated
i the early Church before our Gospels were composed.
onjectures aside, however, there is no real question that
aul's close knowledge of the life and teaching of Jesus came
› him through the witness of the Church, through the
reaching, explanations, and example of those he persecuted,
irough the examination of others before the Sanhedrin, and
irough the fellowship, later, of those who had been with
hrist from the beginning.

This is sufficiently clear from the form of his references
› this fund of knowledge as something "received". It is
irther confirmed by a number of other acknowledged debts
› the Church. Thus, Paul learned soon to interpret Christ's
fe and mission messianically in the light of a certain
lection, and pattern, of Old Testament proof-texts current
i the Church. In the same way, and on the same authority,
e shares with the Church the interpretation of Christ's
eath as sacrificial, making atonement for sin.

He quotes more than once from what were, almost cer-
iinly, early Christian hymns, on the subjects of "the mind
iat was in Christ Jesus", and "God's faithfulness". He
dopts as though entirely his own the title already ascribed
› Jesus by the first disciples, though not so used by the
Iaster Himself, the name of manifold significance — "Lord".
nd he assumes, and frequently uses, as the theme of his
wn counsel to the Churches, "the standard of teaching",
ie "pattern of sound words", the "tradition", which was
i many places the basis of the apostolic education of young
onverts. At many points in his letters, his reliance upon
iis common pattern of moral and religious instruction is
vident: and his unity of purpose and spirit with the existing
hurch is again revealed.

In Paul's experience, as in all others', indebtedness to th Church means in effect indebtedness to certain individu members through whom the total life of the Christian com munity was brought to bear upon his personal situatio Probably the one who contributed most, and was least awar of it, was Stephen, at whose "execution" by a Jewish mo Paul assisted. To him, and to others who bore persecutio with such patience and clear testimony, Paul owed far mor than he could say or they could hope. He owed somethin too, to Ananias, who came to him, albeit reluctantly, in th crucial hour of his conversion, with brotherliness, healin and instruction.

Though Paul later found it necessary, in special circum stances, to deny any subservience to the older apostles, h did not fail to visit Peter, James and John in Jerusalem and shared their fellowship for fifteen days. Someone ha remarked, "They did not for a whole fortnight talk abou the weather!" Silas, who was to become Paul's invaluabl companion, was another of the "leading men among th brethren" whose acquaintance he first made in the earl days at Jerusalem.

It was, however, to Barnabas, once wealthy but now volun tarily impoverished, a trusted and deeply loved leader o the Jerusalem Church, that Paul owed all his later caree When as an ardent young convert Paul "attempted to joi the disciples" at Jerusalem, and met a readily understandabl coolness, suspicion, and fear, it was Barnabas who went fort to speak with him, gave him the right hand of fellowshi brought him to the apostles, and stood guarantor for hi sincerity before the whole Jerusalem Church. The signifi cance of that action defies measurement.

When later Barnabas was sent to Antioch to investigat reports of what to Jewish minds was a strange, unprecedente Christian "outbreak" there, he quickly saw the urgent nee for that unconventional infant Church of pastoral leader ship and instruction, and immediately went off to Tarsu to seek for Paul. So it was again Barnabas who created fo the brilliant convert his first great opportunity for Christia service. Moreover, so far from leaving the younger man t face the difficulties and make his own mistakes uncounselled Barnabas the senior Christian, with Jerusalem's authorit behind him, remained to stand by Paul for a whole year as adviser, supporter, and friend.

And yet again, when in that same Church the call came to adventurous missionary outreach, it was Barnabas and Paul who were sent forth, and only in the course of the first journey did Paul's leadership and intellectual power bring him the ascendancy in the evangelistic team. This is a threefold debt, owed to Barnabas not only by Paul but by the whole Christian Church in every century, which it is impossible to exaggerate.

Yet Stephen, Ananias, Silas and Barnabas are only the first of a very long line of Christian comrades to whose fellowship and co-operation Paul continually pays tribute. All in all, what Paul received from the Church he first persecuted and then served with such passionate zeal, adds up to a considerable sum. Two eloquent and meaningful ordinances, baptism and the Lord's Supper, enshrining the gospel; a clear summary of the faith; considerable knowledge of the sayings, attitudes, character and life of Jesus, of His death and resurrection, and of His gift of the Spirit; the basic conceptions of the Messiahship and sacrifice of Christ; and of love, the kingdom, the Law, the advent, and faith; the existing pattern of instruction for young converts, and the already fashioned catena of Old Testament proof-texts; and innumerable enriching friendships: it all comprises a debt which Paul well knew he could never repay.

Yet he tried. In one great act of his life especially, and one that in the event cost him very dear, for it led directly to his arrest, imprisonment at Caesarea, and appeal to Caesar, he tried to repay. He organised throughout the Gentile Churches a collection of gifts for the sustaining of the impoverished Churches of Judea during severe famine; and while one powerful motive was to demonstrate the unity of Jew and Gentile in Christ, another, urged upon the Romans, is the sense of indebtedness of the whole missionary Church to that mother Church in Palestine. We may be sure Paul felt their spiritual debt was also his own.

Despite all that has been said, or more accurately, because of all that has been said, Paul yet contends earnestly for his spiritual independence as an evangelist, teacher, pastor and apostle, from all merely human authority and commission. A situation arose in which the authenticity of his message, and his standing as a divinely ordained leader of Christ's Church, were thrown in doubt, especially by comparison with those who had been companions of the Lord in Galilee. In defence of all his life-work, and his teaching, Paul protests that he is an apostle "not from men nor through man, but through Jesus Christ and God the Father"; "For I would have you know, brethren, that the gospel which was preached by me is not man's gospel. For I did not receive it from man, nor was I taught it, but it came through a revelation of Jesus Christ." And he carefully explains the limits of his contact with the earlier apostles, to avoid any impression that he was their pupil or protege, and so subject to correction by those who claimed to represent them.

J. S. Stewart remarks that Paul not only claimed independence, "quite obviously he is independent . . . At no time has the Christian Church contained a more original or creative mind." Yet this hardly touches the real issue. Paul denies with equal emphasis that, as to his essential faith and message, he could claim personal originality and creativeness. It was all "received", given, by revelation; it derives from the Lord. Mediated by those in Christ before him, it was nevertheless divinely bestowed and personally authenticated.

The contradiction is merely apparent. What Paul means by "Nor was I taught it, but it came through a revelation of Jesus Christ", he immediately explains by recounting his Judaist upbringing and his Damascus Road experience. This is where he learned the truth, and received both commission and authority. Knowledge, facts, forms, sayings were inherited, but insight, conviction, experience were by revelation. He could join with the men of Samaria in saying, "It is no longer because of your words that we believe, for we have heard for ourselves, and we know that this is indeed the Saviour of the world". He knew what Simon Peter knew at Caesarea Philippi, after many months of watching, listening, learning in the company of the Master-Teacher Himself: the blessedness of an immediate, self-authenticating, irrefutable, divine revelation from the Father in heaven, of the meaning behind the facts and the power within the message – and of who Jesus really was.

And so we meet again in Paul, as in his relation to Jewry,

and his relation to the Graeco-Roman world, a sense both of the greatness, and of the limits, of his indebtedness. Towards those who had given him so much, he ever felt affection and gratitude: yet he knew well that behind them, the ultimate source of all he knew and had experienced, and of his apostleship, was the living Lord Himself. He had grace to appreciate what the Church which gave him birth had bestowed upon him; but he knew that in the end the truth that saves, and the power that transforms, and the love that redeems, are God's alone.

4 *Who Loved Me*

IT IS AN open question whether a man is more accurately "explained" by himself or by his contemporaries. External influences which to an onlooker seem of great importance in the fashioning of any soul, may play their part all unconsciously to the subject himself; while he alone can know the depths from which his inner life is drawn and the forces that impel him to decision and endurance. We may be sure that Paul would place far less emphasis than we do upon his Jewish heritage, Gentile environment, or even Christian encounters, and far more upon the "supra-natural", timeless factors which shaped his life.

The dramatic suddenness of his conversion, seemingly unheralded and unmediated, may partly explain Paul's preoccupation with the over-ruling, sovereign purpose of grace which brought him to Christ. His own faith, like that of his Corinthian converts, stands not in human wisdom or eloquence but in the power of God. All is of grace. We are God's workmanship, and nothing is left to human achievement lest any man should boast.

God has chosen deliberately the foolish, the weak, "things low, and contemptible, things that are nothing", that no flesh should glory in His presence. "It pleased God to reveal his Son to me" is Paul's wondering explanation of the transformation in his life. We obtained salvation "according to the purpose of him who accomplishes all things according to the counsel of his own will"; our experience derives directly from "the eternal purpose which he has realised in Christ Jesus." We are saved by the independent, uncaused self-determination of the sovereign will of God: saved because He chose to save us. It is "of him" that "ye are in Christ Jesus". It is impossible to ignore statements so frequent and so emphatic, whatever questions they may raise in our minds.

God's Will

In the opening chapter of the letter to the Ephesians, the uncompromising assertion of the eternal ground of individual redemption fills the apostle's thought. God is supreme, omniscient, almighty: if men become His children, His redeemed, and His delight, it can never be through something they have done, or have deserved, or brought about, but only because He so purposed, and by His own will brought to pass. Nor could it happen without God's foreknowledge, and consent: man's salvation is neither surprise, nor afterthought, nor accident: "For God knew his own before ever they were, and also ordained that they should be shaped to the likeness of his Son . . . and it is these, so foreordained, whom he has also called."

Behind such insistence lies, of course, the typically Hebrew conception of the majestic sovereignty of God. In the world He made, and which He rules, all is subject at last to His good pleasure: man's freedom is limited, and all the havoc such limited freedom has wrought is subject in the end to God's "Thus far, and no farther . . ." None can impose his will on God; if man finds safety, peace and joy in God, it *can* only be because God has desired him so to do. Thus Paul was certain that behind all the human and historical elements that went to the shaping of his Christian experience, there lay the eternal will of God.

And the moral quality of that timeless will is gracious. Deeper than the ruthless logic is adoring gratitude, "He *loved* me . . ." "By the grace of God I am what I am," he declares; eternal life is the free gift of God, who commended His love toward us in this precise way, that when we were yet without strength, ungodly, still sinners, Christ died for us. All salvation experience is thus traced, in the second place, to sovereign grace, to the unmerited intervention of Him who is rich in mercy and great in love, and to "the exceeding riches of his grace in his kindness toward us in Christ Jesus".

This is the "love of Christ which surpasses knowledge", the perfect patience for the demonstration of which Paul felt he had been especially chosen. Men like Paul, with his record of persecution, and Peter, with his memory of denial, knew that in the deepest analysis they had been saved in spite of themselves. The call of Christ had come to them unsought; grace had besieged their souls, truth hammered their minds, love had wooed their will, before ever they had said "Yes" to Christ. They looked back, not shortsightedly to their choosing of Him but beyond that to His inexplicable, loving, patient, reassuring choice of them. They believed themselves chosen, elect and called, before they had voice or opportunity to answer.

Such, Paul would say, was his greatest debt of all, and the undimmed awareness of it was a vital, and a perpetual, element in Paul's religion. Of course the preaching and hearing of the gospel, believing on Christ with the heart and confessing Him with the mouth, are necessary human steps toward salvation. A man remains responsible for his own reaction to God's purpose for his life. Not a little arrogance, and bewilderment, would have been avoided if the scriptural counsel to "be the more zealous to confirm your call and election" had always been remembered. Whosoever will may come, and if he will not, then he doesn't. But evangelical emphasis upon decision, acceptance, confession of Christ, has sometimes tended to rest salvation upon man's willingness to be saved — whichis absurd — instead of upon God's gracious initiative to save — which is glorious.

Paul's sense of indebtedness here touches the ultimate mystery of all Christian experience. "The word is near you — the word of faith, which we preach"; God has presented His "inexpressible gift", has put forward Christ as an expiation by His blood, has shown His love for us while we were yet sinners; has called and sent the preachers of the good news, all day long holding out His hands with the offer of the gospel — before we knew or cared. And we know within ourselves that all is of God. Behind our struggle is the divine succour, so often undeserved; behind our victory, the divine enabling; behind all our effort at self-reform, the inexplicable new birth that made us want to be different; behind what others call our success, our own wonder that we ever got through. Behind the temptations resisted is the humbling memory of how very nearly we fell — how amazingly we were prevented.

Others may speak kindly of our faith, and fortitude: we know that had it depended upon us, we would have been lost, often and finally. Some inexplicable grace gave unexpected deliverance; God still forgave, when we tasted acute despair. Looking back, we surely know that if we are Christians, it is not by our own faith, or decision, or consecration, but because — with us as with Paul — we were apprehended of Christ Jesus, and He who first confronted, invited, and accepted us has ever since upheld and kept us, in His love.

That is what Paul means. "He destined us in love to be his sons through Jesus Christ, according to the purpose of his will, to the praise of his glorious grace."

Man's Response

If our reaction to this emphasis on the sovereign will of God to save is one of intellectual bewilderment, Paul's was one of boundless and wondering gratitude. The secret of Paul, as W. C. Piggott has said, "the real clue to all his labours is not to be found in his arguments, but in his doxologies, his outbursts of pure wonder at the grace of God, or of almost heart-breaking glory in the cross of our Lord Jesus Christ. 'Oh, the depth of the riches both of the wisdom and of the knowledge of God! How unsearchable are His judgements and His ways past tracing out' ".

An unvarying accent of thankfulness marks Paul's speech. Bursts of praise, ejaculations of thanksgiving, often interrupt intense arguments, delay the rush of thought, welling up irrepressibly from a spirit deeply stirred by the sense of God's immeasurable goodness. Over a score of instances could be listed, and another ten or so occasions when Paul exhorts others to thanksgiving.

The immediate causes of Paul's gratitude have all to do with the grace that saved him and set him within Christ's Church. He records a dozen times his thanksgiving for fellow-Christians, perhaps because his break with his family and race sharpened appreciation of Christian comradeship as one of the great enrichments of the gospel. He thanks God for His "inexpressible gift", perhaps because Pharisaism tended to emphasise that blessing must be purchased by obedience, rather than accepted freely from the overflowing generosity of God.

Paul gave thanks that God leads always those who are in Christ in a ceaseless pageant of triumph – over Satan, over sin, and over death – perhaps because Judaism knew more of struggle than of victory. He would give thanks continually that God has qualified us to share in the inheritance of the saints in light: and again one cannot help comparing the uncertainty and labour of the pious Pharisee seeking to win divine acceptance. He would have the whole Church singing and making melody from the heart, "always and for everything giving thanks in the name of our Lord Jesus Christ to God the Father."

Such is the almost constant level of apostolic experience, the prevailing temper of Pauline Christianity. That all derived from sovereign grace was sufficient reason for a life of overflowing gratitude: "From him, and through him, and to him are all things – to him be glory!" But Paul's insistence that God's gracious initiative was the sole originating cause of our salvation had more far-reaching implications than just a call to Christian thankfulness. It affected deeply Christian thinking; it laid the foundation for Christian life.

To argue, as Paul does, that man's one hope of salvation lies, not in his own achievements, or insight, or enlightened self-interest, but in the redeeming purpose of God that antedates all human effort, and seeks man before he is aware of it, implies an assessment of man's need that is peculiar to Christianity. Human aspiration, endeavour, idealism, receptiveness, all find place in the Christian scheme of human redemption, but only as response to God's gracious will that men be saved, expressed in Him who came to seek and to save that which was lost. Relentlessly Paul (and the whole New Testament) insists that man cannot save himself – not by works of righteousness, not of yourselves, not by the keeping of the Law, nor by charity: but only by penitent faith responding gratefully to the atoning and transforming work of God through Christ.

The collision here between the realism of Paul and the man-centred hope of Humanism cannot be evaded. If indeed "the forces needed for redemption and for the ennobling of life are to be found within man"; if "human control by human effort in accordance with human ideals" can achieve at last a secular paradise, a world man himself has cleansed, an Eden without God; then Paul is wholly wrong. He has exaggerated man's predicament – as helpless until God saves him; and he has misread man's nature, as sinful and dependent, whereas (says Humanism) he is dominant and divine.

The suggestion that Paul has over-stated man's need appears in the light of recent history and of personal experience to be ridiculous, and even frivolous. Only the crassest optimism, blind alike to past failures and to future perils, could build hope for mankind on merely human wisdom directing merely human resources.

As to man's nature, Humanism speaks with two voices. On the one hand, man is dwarfed to insignificance by the measureless backcloth of an expanding universe, by the mindless automatism of historic necessity stemming from accident and blind chance, by uncontrollable and irresponsible social determinations that unconsciously shape his mind and soul, — or by demonic powers rechristened with scientific names. On the other hand, man is exalted as the master of his own fate, his only saviour, self-determining, self-sufficient, and only self-responsible, the "highest" and latest product of an evolution which in him has become self-conscious and therefore self-directing.

Some modern minds find it possible to hold these two incompatible beliefs together; taken alone, each is patently untrue to man's actual situation in the world. In Paul's thought man is both dwarfed and magnified, abased and exalted. Seen against the eternal, cosmic sweep of an unswerving purpose of good, originating in the heart of God the Creator and embracing all that He has made, man is little, and humbled. Yet he is such a creature that purposes so vast and far-reaching have been made to turn upon his choice, response, and co-operation. God, in His sovereign will to save, has chosen not to fulfil His vast designs without including within them man's freedom and responsibility.

The paradox is crucial for the understanding of man: dignity, responsibility, eternal destiny, and a mortal, vulnerable creatureliness are both essential to the human perspective. And Paul's sense of being under God's will the subject and servant of eternal forces, and yet at the same time invited, challenged, to decide, is faithful to the deepest Christian insight into the nature of man, and to the deepest Christian experience.

And Paul's insistence that God's gracious initiative to save is our sole hope of redemption affects no less deeply the whole tone of Christian living. For it provides the foundation, outside oneself, for abiding spiritual assurance of immense value to the struggling soul. There is an inward assurance for the Christian heart, as Paul himself would strongly affirm. "When we cry, 'Abba! Father!' it is the Spirit himself bearing witness with our spirit that we are children of God." There is joy and peace in believing, and new impulses towards new kinds of good are evidence of new life within the soul.

But in Paul's thought, these inner "psychological" grounds of spiritual assurance are balanced by the "objective" theological truth that it is God's will that saves us, and not our feelings, or even our faith by itself. The Christian is thus turned outwards from himself to contemplate events and purposes larger than his own conceiving, and dependent on far more than his own will. Christ *has* come, and lived, and died, and risen again; in the gospel the grace of God has reached his heart through the historic Church. He, like Paul, can appeal beyond the fluctuating moods of self-assurance to the deeper, undergirding truth of God's intention to save him, and the fact of the divine intervention in his life. Our salvation is the Lord's doing, and it is marvellous in our eyes.

The logic of sovereign grace argues that since God did not begin to love us because of what we were, He will go on loving us in spite of what we are. Refusing to speculate on the position of others, or to rest a slothful and complacent soul on mere spiritual conceit, the Christian yet knows that he is "in Christ" because God set him there: and that "He who began a good work . . . will bring it to completion at the day of Jesus Christ."

Such humble confidence, built not upon our inconstant feelings but upon God's constant will, spells for the Christian freedom, peace, endurance, and joy. A tense, inward-turning, endlessly self-searching pietism can be an unhealthy and unlovely thing; Paul's bold affirmations point the way to an extravert evangelicalism that is strong, positive, assured, and compellingly grateful, resting all the future in the love that will not let us go. This, Paul would say, is my security: that before I knew Him, He foreknew, fore-ordained, loved, chose and called me – and gave Himself *for me!*

Paul the Convert

Wretched Man That I Am!

As I Journeyed

Members One of Another

5 *Wretched Man That I Am!*

It is at first sight very strange that Gamaliel's brilliant student should have imbibed so little of the wise and patient statesmanship of his revered tutor, at any rate in his attitude towards "the sect of the Nazarenes". For with true Pharisaic confidence in the over-ruling providence of God, Gamaliel advised the Sanhedrin, "Take care what you do with these men . . . let them alone; for if this plan or this undertaking is of men, it will fail; but if it is of God, you will not be able to overthrow them. You might even be found opposing God!"

But Paul will have none of this temporising neutrality. In the deliberations of the Sanhedrin, when Christians were on trial, he cast his vote for death. He took a personal, if passive, interest in the stoning of the first Christian martyr, Stephen, "consenting to his death". Personal hostility widened into a violent campaign of persecution: "Saul laid waste the Church, and entering house after house he dragged off men and women and committed them to prison."

Nor was this a merely judicial assessment of public necessity, impartially and reluctantly accepted. In Paul's own words: "I punished them often in all the synagogues and tried to make them blaspheme; and in raging fury against them, I persecuted them even to foreign cities."

"In raging fury": that confession illumines Luke's description. "Saul, still breathing threats and murder against the disciples of the Lord, went to the high priest and asked him for letters to the synagogues at Damascus so that if he found any belonging to the Way, men or women, he might bring them bound to Jerusalem."

The impatience of youth, and the obvious failure of more moderate policies to stem the growing Christian contagion, doubtless help to explain Paul's passion against the Church. Yet it remains strange that against so weighty advice, and despite the former official restraint, he should personally take the lead in stirring up energetic and relentless antagonism towards a movement which — he would say — embraced only ignorant and unlearned men, deluded by a fanatical peasant into messianic excitement, and declaring incredible nonsense about a resurrection from the dead.

Paul's evident sincerity — "I myself was convinced that I

ought to do many things in opposing the name of Jesus of Nazareth . . ." — places him among those of whom Jesus had said, "The hour is coming when whoever kills you will think he is offering service to God". But even so, his ruthlessness, his consuming conviction, his relentless pursuit of the scattering disciples, betray a state of mind that challenges further explanation.

In Paul's own account of the moment when this headlong career of violence was suddenly halted, there is a revealing reference to a prolonged resistance to continual prompting. The figure is that of a stubborn ox lashing out furiously against the painful jabs of a goad skilfully applied to the tenderest areas of flesh, vigorously resisting the instructions thereby conveyed and venting its wild anger in a display of threatening violence against its master. Paul himself said it! — and no picture could better convey the helpless fury of a mind determined to stifle the insidious whisper of unwelcome truth.

The outward violence against the Church reflects, and partially purges, the inward tumult of one unsure of himself despite all his privileged background and intense training, unsure of the ultimate triumph of the faith he held, unsure of his own feelings, and already becoming angrily aware of the futility of combating ideas with force.

Years later, writing to the Church at Philippi, the persecutor, now himself persecuted, dramatically reveals something of what he was feeling as he journeyed to Damascus. He urges the Philippians not to be frightened in any thing by their opponents, and adds the illuminating comment: this fearlessness under persecution "is clear omen to them of their destruction, but of your salvation, and that from God." The Christian's unresenting fortitude, such as Paul had witnessed in Stephen, was itself the evidence that Christians possessed something their persecutors lacked; the spirit they showed was self-evidently "from God", and the effect on the persecutor was to reinforce misgivings and prompt disturbing questions as to which, in the end, was heading for "destruction".

By the time of his own imprisonment, Paul had learned how effectively the attempt to suppress Christianity by force "really served to advance the gospel"; but already on the road to Damascus we can discern the symptoms of a mind shaken with doubt, burdened by inner conflict, haunted with guilt-feelings about his own inner life, and unable to explain away to his own satisfaction the faith and courage of those he so mercilessly hunted. The clear "omen of destruction" was already plain to the persecutor's conscience.

Disillusion

That this interpretation is neither fanciful nor forced is shown by Paul's later references to his spiritual pilgrimage. The realistic assessment of the failures of Judaism which mingled with his love of his people and its faith is not wholly post-conversion. As we saw, such misgivings about Jewish character and reputation were shared by others, including several existing Reform-sects, and were especially strong within Pharisaic circles. Moreover, although much must be allowed to later Christian clarification, it would appear that Paul was already aware that such failures were not exceptional or accidental, but symptomatic of real deficiencies in the Jewish faith.

To Paul, the central issue in all religion was the attainment of righteousness in the sight of God. Although this was primarily a *status* of acceptance with the Most High, a covenanted relationship guaranteeing the continuance of divine mercies here and hereafter, it could not be divorced, for any Pharisee, from a *state* of righteousness achieved by obedience to the multitudinous commandments of the Law. Paul could indeed claim to be, "as to righteousness under the Law, blameless." But his heart was not satisfied, his conscience unsilenced. With another, in a very similar case, he could say, "All these things have I observed from my youth", and still feel constrained to ask, "What must I do to inherit eternal life . . . What do I still lack?"

Paul had found no answer. To his mature mind, having a righteousness of one's own, based on the Law, was no longer possible as a way of human salvation. He relinquished even the hope of such self-redemption, accepting instead a free gift of righteousness, "the righteousness from God" that depends, not on perfect obedience, but upon faith in Jesus Christ.

This far-reaching abandonment of Judaism's main thesis and promise is most vigorously argued in Paul's letter to the Galatians, and more systematically defended in the letter to the Romans. And at first one wonders that the apostle argues so vehemently a question that after all is somewhat academic and theological, a dispute about the theory of religion rather than about vital issues of experience and life.

But this impression is suddenly dispelled when we reach the heart of the Roman letter, and a passage full of the tensions and disappointments that clouded the apostle's own personal decision against Judaism and for Christ. We might have suspected, from the way the Galatian letter opens with memories of his conversion, that the arguments against Judaism had painful associations for Paul: Romans 7 makes it certain.

Said T. R. Glover: "There are those who do not read autobiography in the seventh chapter of Romans – as if Paul used the first person singular here in the style practised by rhetoricians of the second order – as if such writing could be anything but autobiography!" Admittedly, it is a little more debateable whether this illuminating self-revelation belongs properly to pre-conversion or to post-conversion experience: the truth seems to be that while the writing certainly bears evidence of later Christian reflection, the experience described could scarcely be accepted as typical of one who had found salvation and peace in Christ. In Denney's phrase, Romans 7 represents Paul's pre-conversion life "seen through regenerate eyes", and together with Paul's indictment of Judaism's failures, and his confession of not having found righteousness by the Law, it sufficiently explains the "chaos and frenzy of his mind" in the days before Damascus. There are indeed painful, even poignant, memories behind the vehemence of his argument with those who would lead his young Galatian converts back to the unsatisfying bondage of Jewish legalism.

Precisely wherein Paul felt he had so dismally failed, and Judaism had failed him, is not defined. The value of the Jewish Law, which was ever in his eyes "holy and just and good", indeed "spiritual", lay in establishing the ideal towards which men should strive, the standard by which to measure attainment, and the promise of "life" implied – in which, he could say, "in my inmost self, I delight". But the Law could offer no moral inspiration, no resources of spiritual power, sufficient to subdue that other "force" – or "rule" – of sinful desire, which "dwelling in me, that is, in my flesh," makes me "captive to the law of sin which dwells in my members."

This psychological civil war between reason and emotion, conscience and lust, self-indulgence and self-discipline, "flesh" and "spirit", is familiar in all moral teaching. It prompted Plato's picture of the rearing and plunging horses that drag the chariot of the soul upwards and downwards simultaneously, demanding the utmost strength and skill of the reasonable will, the charioteer. It is behind Bunyan's account of the assault upon the city of Mansoul. It is portrayed again in the myth of Orpheus with his lute captivating the senses of the sailors lest they hear the siren voices that lure to destruction – the true and the false beauty contending for the souls of men.

For many in our time, it is the moral beauty and supreme challenge of Jesus Himself which first awakens in the growing soul an awareness of holy things, and because of repeated failure and remorse, a realisation of sin's power and subtlety For Paul, it was the Jewish Law which thus revealed the slavery of the flesh to sin: "I am carnal, *sold* under sin", so that "I do not do what I want, but I do the very thing I hate . . . I can will what is right, but I cannot do it. For I do not do the good I want, but the evil I do not want is what I do . . . When I want to do right, evil lies close at hand . . . Wretched man that I am! Who will deliver me from this body of death?"

Ay and for me there shot from the beginning
Pulses of passion broken with my breath;
Oh thou poor soul, enwrapped in such a sinning,
Bound in the shameful body of thy death!

Well, let me sin, but not with my consenting,
Well, let me die, but willing to be whole:
Never, O Christ, – so stay me from relenting, –
Shall there be truce betwixt my flesh and soul.

Paul found his answer in Christ. "The rule of the Spirit of life in Christ Jesus has set me free from the rule of sin and death" – Paul uses the word "law" for a power or principle that rules the soul, whether the ruling principle of the Jewish Law, which failed, or the ruling principle of sin, which enslaved him, or the ruling principle of the

Spirit which set him free and gave him "life". "God has done [through Christ] what the Law, weakened by the flesh, could not do". The Law pointed to the ideal; it could not enable men to fulfil it – that was Judaism's failure, and Paul's personal tragedy.

References to "the flesh" and to "the law of sin in the members" inevitably suggest that the particular sphere of failure was the realm of sexual morality, and there are other indications in Paul's letters that this might have been so. Yet we must not restrict the personal sense of failure, or the disillusionment with Judaism, to any one area of experience. As C. H. Dodd remarks, "It is highly significant that Paul has chosen for his example the one prohibition of the Decalogue which deals with the inner life, and not with overt action." Significant indeed, for Paul has placed his finger upon the same weak spot in legalism that Jesus exposed in the Sermon on the Mount: "Thou shalt not covet . . ." is concerned with the same moral problem as Jesus' prohibition of *wanting* to do wrong.

Law generally can deal only with actions, as they can be witnessed and judged by others; morality and religion must take account also of motive, intention, desire, temptation, the state of soul behind the act, and sometimes the state of soul without the act (the mere look of lust, the desire to kill, the attitude of contempt, to cite Christ's three examples) when circumstances, or cowardice, prevent the sinful desire being manifest in deeds. So legal enactments can only regulate behaviour; they cannot produce saints. The finest qualities of the human spirit – the fruits in human life of the presence of the Holy Spirit – belong in a realm "where there is no law".

Only the total regeneration of the soul by the indwelling of a wholly new spirit can accomplish the inward righteousness God demands. Jeremiah and Ezekiel had long ago declared this: Paul learned it in experience, to the point of near-despair. And the nagging consciousness of his own secret failures, and of the inability of Pharisaism to help him find peace and harmony of soul – contrasted with the obvious joy, courage and peace of the Christians he was hounding to their death – constituted the sharp, infuriating goads against which his spirit rebelled as he rode with violence to Damascus.

To emphasise how long and how deeply the soul of Paul was strafed by the truth concerning himself, concerning his ancestral faith, and concerning the Christians he persecuted, before that final Damascus bombshell burst within his life, is not to minimise for a moment the wonder of that astonishing conversion. It is merely to pay heed to the man's own testimony long afterwards, to appreciate more accurately the forces pent up within his personality for Christ to release in tireless zeal, and to rescue the conversion-story from sheer magic. But it underlines, in addition, how very much we modern Christians have still to learn about the spiritual "technique" of evangelism.

In his repellent, yet important and timely study of the "psychological mechanisms" of brain-washing, political persuasion, forcible confession, and religious conversion (entitled "Battle for the Mind") W. A. Sargant, physician in psychological medicine at a well-known London teaching hospital declares, amid many challenging and unwelcome things: "Those who wish to disperse wrong beliefs and undesirable behaviour-patterns, and afterwards implant saner beliefs and attitudes, are more likely to achieve success if they can first induce some degree of nervous tension, or stir up sufficient feelings of anger or anxiety, to secure the person's undivided attention and possibly increase his suggestibility. By increasing or prolonging stresses . . . a more thorough alteration of the person's thinking processes may be achieved."

Sargant adduces a wealth of illustration from the Journal of John Wesley, of the intense mental and even physical distress produced in some of Wesley's hearers, preparatory to their finding peace in Christ. He speaks of Wesley's discovery that habits are changed most easily by "a tremendous assault upon the emotions", and adds the significant comment: "All evidence goes to show that there can be no new Protestant revival while the policy continues of appealing mainly to adult intelligence and reason, and until Church leaders consent to take more advantage of the normal person's emotional mechanism, for disrupting old behaviour patterns and implanting new."

This is a spiritual lesson in strange terms, and from an unexpected source, and set amid some very strange judgements and arguments: but there can be little doubt that this particular comment is justified. It is undeniable that great religious revivals and new spiritual movements within the Church are always assocated with deep emotional stresses — sometimes with emotional excesses -- and that until the hearer is disturbed, his armour of complacency pierced, his pride undone, by a sense of need, or fear, or self-reproach, or shame, the careful exposition of truth will not catch fire within the soul nor accomplish its saving work.

None will want to create emotional distress where no reason for it already exists: an artificial fear, or shame, or anxiety can mean nothing for genuine conversion. But words of the great American evangelist Finney are apposite: "Some people fear to press a point to which the mind is tremblingly alive, lest they should injure the mind . . . You should clear up the point, throw the light of truth all round it, and bring the soul to yield, and then the mind is at rest."

Spurious emotionalism and short-lived decisions are unworthy of Christ: but we can become too intellectualist, and forget that emotion is only what "moves". If the fear of hell and an oppressive sense of personal guilt seem impossible to most modern people, yet war, anxiety, self-antagonism, disintegrating neuroses, the hangovers of outraged conscience when the spree has passed, domestic insecurities, insupportable responsibilities, poisonous complexes and the mental sickness of unpurged memories, unsilenced self-accusations, and unharmonised drives, all abound beneath the surface of our sophisticated society; and each disguises with a polished and modern-sounding name an old malady to which the healing grace of Christ specifically applies.

We must learn from Paul's experience to speak to man's condition, to plough up the complacent soul and root beneath the trodden emotions of our artificial age, until once again spiritual nerves respond to the realities of life, the moral law, and death, responsibility to God and final judgement. For none can be saved until they know, and feel, that they are lost; and none are so near redemption as those who cry with Paul in near-despair "Wretched man that I am, who will deliver me?"

6 *As I Journeyed*

Out of the many thousands of conversions in Christian history, only one — that of Paul — is celebrated with an appointed Feast Day in the Church's calendar. Next to the birth, death, and resurrection of Jesus and the Day of Pentecost, it is of course the most significant event in the New Testament story, and nothing in the subsequent history of the Church parallels its importance for all time and for all the world.

That brief but astonishing encounter outside Damascus won for Jesus His most attentive disciple, His greatest apostle, His most devoted servant. It removed at one stroke the Church's ablest and most violent enemy. It gave to Christianity her most valiant champion, her most brilliant leader, her profoundest thinker, her most ardent evangelist, one of her most attractive saints. It made possible the rich legacy of his writings for the counsel and encouragement of all later centuries. It defines, more clearly than any doctrine, the essential purpose and meaning of the gospel, and it demonstrates with inescapable force the divine power that is at work in Christianity.

For Paul's experience provides impressive illustration of Christian conversion achieved in the hardest circumstances and on the most difficult level. If we may say that Zaccheus exemplifies a conversion mainly moral in quality, from dishonest avarice to penitent generosity, with all which that implies; and Nicodemus exemplifies a conversion mainly intellectual, a new birth of spiritual understanding; and Mary Magdalene a conversion mainly emotional, a cleansing liberation from defilement that made possible new and sanctified life; then — with similar one-sided emphasis — we may say that Paul's was a conversion essentially "religious", though of course that term embraces intellectual, moral, and emotional factors, too. And the conversion of the religious is the greatest miracle of grace!

Of the young Pharisee's zeal for God it is needless to say more: his learning in Judaist lore, his scrupulousness, his aggressive earnestness, were outstanding. Of his racial pride, as a true Hebrew of the royal tribe of Benjamin, it is only necessary to recall that all the fierce nationalism of a conquered people, the pride of a matchless history, the boast of divine election, were in him intensified by a strict Pharisaic training. Of his rising fame, we need only remember his position as Rabbi, member of the Sanhedrin, accredited representative of Jerusalem's authority to Damascus. Moreover, he was publicly and passionately committed to convictions which could only be repudiated at a severe cost of mental anguish, loss of face, and accusations of betrayal.

Adding these together, it would be natural to conclude that such a man could not be stopped; that a character shaped by such circumstances could not be changed. For religious bigotry, fanatic nationalism, intellectual commitment and forging ambition are surely among the strongest drives that can possess a man. United in one personality they seem irresistible. Yet this man exchanged his proud and ancient religion for the despised creed of a hunted coterie of obscure folk; his ardent, racialist nationalism for a world-wide dream of brotherhood: and a glorious career amid admiration, scholarly repute, increasing power, and great wealth, for a friendless, arduous, poverty-haunted life, doubly despised as renegade and as Christian.

Miracle indeed!

The Event

Inward turmoil and growing disillusionment apart, what brought Paul to that shattering earthquake of experience was essentially a personal confrontation. Paul came face to face with the Jesus he already knew about, but did not know.

The form of the experience resembled that of an Old Testament theophany. A manifestation of divine glory, as light flashing suddenly from heaven, above the brightness of "noon" and "brighter than the sun", was accompanied by a voice speaking the Hebrew language and bearing a divine communication. Others saw the light, and (apparently) heard the sound, but did not distinguish articulate speech. All fell prostrate, and there ensued a colloquy like that of God with Moses at the burning bush, and of God with Isaiah within the Temple. Further instructions are promised, to be given by more normal means, and the central figure bears for days a physical consequence of the event, in blindness – as Jacob limped after wrestling with God at Peniel, and Moses' face shone after communing with God at Sinai.

Despite this Old Testament form, the atmosphere of Paul's experience is nearer to that of the first Easter Day. All is light, wonder, even fear; the deepest, most permanent, result is the unshakeable conviction of Paul that he had seen the Lord. Reciting the resurrection-appearances of Jesus, to Cephas, to the Twelve, to the five hundred, and to James, Paul adds: "Last of all . . . he appeared also to me." Paul's conversion is indeed the latest of the resurrection stories.

The precise nature of Paul's experience we may leave to the psychologists to debate, if they can; Paul himself calls it a "heavenly vision". What cannot be explained away is the total and permanent transformation of the young persecuting Pharisee, in belief, in character, in ambition, in his whole personality; nor the burning conviction, that never wavered or hesitated thereafter, that Jesus was risen and Jesus was Lord, the Christ of God.

This is the very heart of the event, the revelation of Jesus of Nazareth as alive, as divine and glorified, as somehow identified with His followers in their suffering, and therefore as undoubtedly Lord. These are precisely the notes of the primitive gospel: Paul is brought immediately to the crucial confession required of all converts, that Jesus is Christ, the Lord. "Saul, Saul, why . . . ?" sets Paul at once upon the defensive, and evokes the decisive answer, "Who are you, *Lord?*" with, a moment later, "What shall I do, Lord?" With those two questions every Christian life begins.

The crisis was sudden, but the total experience lasted three days. Paul was a convert of unusual calibre, and it cannot be doubted that he knew the faith he persecuted. Yet even he must take time to assimilate and clarify the staggering revelation that has come to him. Contact with the Church (in the person of Ananias) and further instruction in the faith were required of Paul as they were of all other converts in apostolic days. Luke certainly does not mean that Ananias had no more to say than is recorded.

Paul himself in later years comments upon his blindness, and upon the falling from his eyes of "something like scales" as the full truth dawns upon him, by declaring that when a man turns to the Lord "the veil is removed". Perhaps a similar reminiscence of his own obstinate unbelief sharpens the words: "the god of this world has blinded the minds of the unbelievers, to keep them from seeing *the light of the gospel of the glory of Christ.*" That final phrase perfectly describes what broke upon Paul's soul outside Damascus.

With illumination came enduement with the Holy Spirit; as conversion reached its culmination in Christian baptism. And the witness to Christ begun in baptism was pursued in public preaching in the synagogues of Damascus. In what way, and with what power, the Spirit was with him became immediately evident in the amazement and "confounding" of all who heard.

By a curious coincidence, Luke says these things began "as he journeyed"; Paul tells the Jerusalem crowd that it happened "as I made my journey"; and again to Agrippa Paul fixes the important moment with the phrase "Thus I journeyed . . ." A sense of being abruptly halted in mid-career, almost of being tripped up and overthrown, seems associated in Paul's memory with that great day. So his namesake the son of Kish (also of the tribe of Benjamin) had once gone out upon a journey to seek his father's asses, had unexpectedly met Samuel, and had found a kingdom. Paul went out upon a journey seeking the scattering Christians, had suddenly met Jesus, and had found the kingdom of God.

The Consequences

The three days stretched into three years. Long afterwards Paul reveals that he went away into Arabia (the Nabataean kingdom east of Damascus), then returned to Damascus, and only went up again to Jerusalem "after three years". The fact is stated defensively, as the alternative to conferring "with flesh and blood . . . those who were apostles before me". All that human counsel could offer him he had already received. So revolutionary were the new insights gained in the Damascus Road revelation that it was imperative "to think through their implications and to reconstruct around them the edifice of his religious belief" in comparative solitude and the presence of God.

Yet it is possible to trace, to some extent and tentatively, the lines which his mental, moral, and emotional re-adjustment must have followed. The first and greatest effort must have been to accustom his mind to the truth that the long-awaited Messiah had come. This he now knew, for he had seen the risen Master; and (as he told the Roman Christians afterwards) Jesus was clearly "designated Son of God in power according to the Spirit of holiness by his resurrection from the dead – Jesus Christ our Lord". But the knowledge turned his whole world upside down. The Jewish dream had been fulfilled, the ancient prophecies had come true; Paul's gaze must henceforth be focussed not only forwards upon a distant hope but also backwards upon Messiah's first advent among the chosen race. That alone demanded fundamental re-thinking.

But Messiah had been rejected, put to shame, crucified. The unthinkable had happened. Israel had been entirely mistaken, her picture of Messiah all wrong. Moving and mysterious passages in books of the later prophets, telling of one who should be God's Servant, who should be despised and rejected of men, a man of sorrows, bruised, smitten, afflicted, and who in the end should give his life a ransom for many, suddenly took on startling and vivid meaning.

The ancient institution of atoning sacrifice, redeeming life by life-giving, and purging sin by the shedding of blood, now became more significant than ever – an agelong education in the principles by which God could redeem mankind through vicarious suffering. Jesus was the Christ, and yet crucified: because Jesus was the Servant-Messiah, a Ransom, a Sacrifice, and a Saviour.

So the promised kingdom was here – as a kingdom of righteousness, peace, and joy in the Holy Ghost. The long-heralded Day of the Lord had dawned, as a day of salvation. In the fulness of God's time a new time had begun, the acceptable year of the Lord. All the hopes of Hebrew poets and prophets had been fulfilled, not as foreseen but far more gloriously. It was all new, astonishing; to a mind with Paul's training it was revolutionary: and Paul never lost the wonder of the surprising news that made his gospel.

But, thirdly, if Israel had been wrong, so had he. Much that he had lived for, and lived by, was totally devalued. What mattered his Rabbinic lore if its foundation, and its whole system of interpretation, was mistaken? What was pride of race, if the race had rejected its destiny, and stood in peril of being itself rejected? What remained of his own confidence in Hebrew ancestry, Pharisaic zeal, and blameless righteousness by the Law's standard, when he had persecuted Messiah's people? All hope of acceptance with God was swept away in the overwhelming conviction that he had been disastrously wrong, fighting against God.

Paul's revulsion was violent and complete. "Whatever gain I had," he writes in after years, "I counted loss for Christ." He never again doubted that all he had valued and built upon in religion was worthless. "Indeed, I count everything as loss because of the surpassing worth of knowing Christ Jesus my Lord. For his sake I have suffered the loss of all things, and count them as refuse, in order that I may gain Christ . . ." So to renounce all confidence in himself and his achievements, in inherited privilege and divine favouritism, in rank and knowledge and personal merit, was a shattering step for any Jew to take. It is shattering for any man. But conversion to Christ as Saviour demands it.

Involved in this step was a total reversal of thought concerning what is central, and determinative, in all religion. To Paul hitherto it had been righteousness, before God and before men, achieved by scrupulous observance of the Law, and entitling a man to divine favour and reward. That, in his own case and for many of his compatriots, this religion of moral effort spurred by legal sanctions had failed, did not for a moment invalidate its divine authority. The fault lay with man's sinful nature. But now all is changed. The focus of his new faith was not a precept but a Person, not a written Law but a living Spirit, not obedience to a set of abstract principles but passionate loyalty to One honoured, and trusted, and loved beyond all others.

In the glow of this new revelation, men placed their faith implicitly in Christ, the Servant, the Crucified, the Lord, and found joy and power and moral transformation and fortitude. They counted it honour to suffer for His name; willingly, like Stephen, they died for Him. This devotion to Messiah was a new principle in religion, one that was proving its power to save – in Paul as in others. Not under the Law but "in Christ" was salvation to be found; and to be "in Christ", possessing not one's own righteousness but that which was God's free gift to all who were "in Him", was to be – already – accepted with God. Yet the divine Law, never abrogated, was being fulfilled after all, as the

Spirit of Christ changed him gradually into the image of his Lord. So wonderful was the whole tenor and spirit and joy of this new religious life of freedom and confidence in a Messiah who was also Saviour and Lord, that it seemed to Paul (as he told the Galatians) that only those who were fools, or bewitched, would ever contemplate returning to the bondage of Judaism.

It seems probable that another aspect of Paul's re-adjustment is reflected in a certain progress of thought discernible in the three accounts of his conversion. In the first, Ananias is persuaded to visit the arch-persecutor by the assurance that "he is a chosen instrument of mine to carry my name before the Gentiles and kings and the sons of Israel; for I will show him how much he must suffer for the sake of my name." In the second account, Ananias says to Paul, "You will be a witness for him to all men . . ." In the third, the Lord says, "I have appeared to you for this purpose, to appoint you to serve and bear witness . . . delivering you from the people and from the Gentiles — to whom I send you . . ."

So is recorded the growing realisation just how completely conversion was to transform Paul's whole career. His fervent devotion to conserving the ancient, exclusive privileges of his race must now give place to a cosmopolitan universalism which shall offer the good news of Messiah to all who will believe. Suffering, labour, misunderstanding, peril, will not be harder to accept than this direct reversal of all former convictions. Yet he accepts the commission without reserve, and all treasured habits of thought, expectations, and ambitions are renounced in ready obedience to his new Master's will.

A Messiah come, a Messiah crucified, all confidence in self destroyed, and religion itself transformed, all life's plans, convictions and ideals dissolved to be revalued and rebuilt: such were some of the consequences of Paul's encounter with Christ — who Himself changes not, but who mightily changes all who come to Him.

The Reflections

Nevertheless, important though the re-adjustments were, the event itself was the amazing thing. The mechanics of the matter may be analysed at will: the fact, in all its inexplicable paradox, remains. The stubborn Pharisee is turned upon his tracks, the fierce pride is humbled, the partisan fury and nationalist zeal are quenched; the champion of Jewry becomes leader of the Church, and one against whom many devout hearts had earnestly prayed became one for whom thousands, of his own and subsequent generations, can never sufficiently thank God.

Paul's own reflections on the event emphasise chiefly this miraculous nature of its underlying cause. It is tempting to suspect a wry play upon words when he speaks of being "apprehended" of Christ Jesus – laid hold of, overtaken and violently seized: the phrase well describes his own experience, the pursuer of others himself pursued, the arrestor arrested! Such a sense of divine compulsion accompanies every true conversion.

In an ambiguous phrase, "God was pleased to reveal his Son in me", Paul fastens upon revelation as the central factor in the total event that changed him. We are reminded of Christ's comment upon Peter's first confession of His Sonship, that such insight had been given by the Father Himself. Every convert knows that whereas he was blind now he sees; that he possesses a faith which no man can destroy because it comes, in the last resort, directly to the heart from God.

Among Paul's metaphors for conversion are four which dramatise the miracle of new beginning. He likens the experience to the first, primeval day: "It is the God who said 'Let light shine out of darkness' who has shone in our hearts to give the light of the knowledge of the glory of God in the face of Christ". To Agrippa, to the Colossians, to the Ephesians and to the Thessalonians Paul uses the same figure, of being transported by Christ from darkness to light, and made "sons of light". The frequent allusion leaves no doubt that Paul so saw his own conversion, as a marvellous, creative illumination of life and death, of past, present, and future, of man and God – the light of the glory of Christ breaking into his soul as the first light had broken across the darkened void when creation began.

So, "if any one is in Christ, he is a new creation; the old has passed away, behold the new has come." Nothing avails, Paul tells the Galatians, but a new creation; and he exhorts the Colossians to manifest the new nature, renewed in them after the image of its Creator. "We are his workmanship, created in Christ Jesus . . ."

Paul's second dramatic metaphor is birth, or adoption. The Corinthians are "babes", the Galatians, "my little children, with whom I am again in travail", and Onesimus, "my child, whose father I have become in my imprisonment". Here the thought is of immaturity and affectionate relationship, but "regeneration and renewal of the Holy Ghost" is not far from Paul's mind. His more usual way of describing entry into the family of God, however, is by the analogy of "adoption" – because in Roman society, with its slavery and concubinage, acknowledgement as one of the family, by the father, was in fact more important than physical parentage. Christians receive the adoption of sons, possess the Spirit of adoption, are no longer slaves but sons, and so heirs. "In Christ Jesus you are all sons of God, through faith." Whether by adoption or by birth, by the Father's will we are members of His family, and after the bondage of Judaism, the terrors of paganism, that is miraculous in itself!

Paul's third metaphor of miraculous beginnings is resurrection. We have died and risen again with Christ. Writing to the Romans, and again to the Colossians, Paul expounds baptism as a sharing together in Christ's death to sin, in His burial, and in His resurrection to "newness of life". In the letter to the Ephesians this idea is repeated without the baptismal overtones: we were dead in sin, and God has made us alive in Christ. The contrast of the unchristian past with our new life in Christ could not be more startlingly represented: by faith we adhere to Christ, who died and rose again – therefore we die and rise with Him. That is conversion. Paul the Pharisee died on the Damascus Road, and Paul the apostle and evangelist rose phoenix-like from the dust!

The fourth dramatic metaphor recalls the exodus of Israel from Egypt. We give thanks to the Father who "has qualified us to share in the inheritance of the saints . . . has delivered us from the dominion of darkness and transferred us to the kingdom of his beloved Son, in whom we have redemption . . ." To Christians, as to Israel, has come divine deliverance: Christ, greater than Moses, has brought liberation, endowing life with a new freedom, transferring life to a new realm, and lighting up life with a new prospect. We have been baptised unto Christ as Israel was to Moses "in the cloud and in the sea", and we, too, have drunk from the supernatural Rock, which was Christ.

In each of these expressions the emphasis falls upon the same truth: in divine arrest, or revelation, in creation, birth, or resurrection, or in divine deliverance, it is the word and hand and power of God that operates. Of his own experience and of ours, Paul would say that by whatever means it was accomplished, only God could do it. Not only the Church felt that Paul's transformation was a miracle: Paul felt it so himself, and never ceased to wonder.

The miracle was not only one of power, but of mercy. It was for His great love wherewith He loved us, and because He is rich in mercy, that God had shown His hand. This, also, is inexplicable. "He saved us, not because of deeds done by us in righteousness, but in virtue of his own mercy." And Paul will press that truth to the edge of making mercy an absolute, unchallengeable prerogative of Deity: "I will have mercy on whom I have mercy, and I will have compassion on whom I have compassion. So it depends not upon man's will or exertion but upon God's mercy . . . So then he has mercy upon whomever he wills."

We shall not begin to understand Paul's life unless we realise that for him conversion was sheer miracle – a miracle of grace.

7 *Members One of Another*

It is not surprising that Paul's application to join the Church at Jerusalem was challenged. Christians had good reason to be cautious, and his professed conversion – so hard to credit – could have been a ruse to gain information for a further campaign of repression. It needed the grace of Barnabas to overcome their natural hesitation.

What is surprising, at any rate to some schools of evangelical Christianity, is that after such rebuff Paul should persist in his attempt to be accepted among the Jerusalem Christians. Luke does not use the more common expression "sought to join", but something nearer to "endeavoured to join", a turn of phrase which he also uses of the "endeavouring" to preach in Bithynia, which was frustrated, and the "endeavouring" to profane the Temple, which the Jews claimed they had prevented. In each case, persistence seems implied; certainly Paul sustained his application long enough to be at last welcomed in the Jerusalem fellowship.

This serves as a small but significant clue to a large area of Paul's thinking. Paul already knew much about the infant Church, its immaturity, its uncertainties, its internal stresses, its lack of organisation. He knew that its leadership consisted mainly of "uneducated, common men", and its membership of some very poor folk whom the rich had to maintain. He knew – none knew better – how persecution had scattered the original disciples, and how few altogether the Christians were.

Moreover, did he need to join the Church at all? He had already received a stupendous revelation. He had seen the Lord, as many of the Church had not. His life had been transformed without their aid. He had received a commission from Christ, and needed no man's ordination; and in any case his training, gifts and originality reinforced a strongly independent mind.

And yet, with no illusions about the Church, and with a tremendous spiritual experience behind him, Paul pressed for admission. He might conceivably have become an independent itinerant evangelist, self-appointed, self-advertised, self-sufficient, "answerable only to the Lord". He could have gathered around him a conclave of spiritual cronies and formed some new "cell" or society or brotherhood – as nearly happened with Peter and Apollos among the foolish Corinthians.

But Paul would have none of it. He would join the existing, fallible, despised Church at Jerusalem, and press his application to acceptance. Our only clues to the reasons which prompted this insistence lie in his later teaching: we must assume that what in after years he urged upon others, merely made articulate ideas about the Church of Christ which he had already begun to understand during his discipline of re-assessment in Arabia.

The Body

Instructing his own converts, Paul later insisted that the organised Church on earth, the Church existing in Jerusalem, Antioch, Ephesus, Corinth, Rome, and elsewhere, was the living "incarnation" of the Spirit of Jesus. At the outset of his own Christian experience, on the Damascus Road itself, he had discovered that whoso touches the Church touches Christ: "Saul, Saul," the Lord had said, "why do you persecute *me?*" Perhaps even earlier he had recognised, in the way Stephen died, in his courage, and radiance, and gentle forgivingness, the Spirit ascribed to Jesus Himself. Wherever the conception began, it became Paul's controlling thought about the Church: she is the Body in which Christ dwells.

So commonplace has this idea grown that we remember with real surprise that to speak of being a "member" of the Church is to use a somewhat gruesome, anatomical metaphor. It is probable that Paul was not the first in history to use this figure of a "corporate" or body-like society of individuals "organically united"; but in his thought it became an effective reply to the quarrelsomeness and self-centredness of some Christians at Corinth. Their mutual dependence in spiritual experience, their necessary sharing of one life of God pulsing through them all, their "wholeness" though each part differs in function within the whole, is likened by Paul to the unity of ear, eye, hand and foot in one human body. The several organs (or "members") can neither disparage each other, nor function properly without each other, nor can the body – if it is to remain healthy and whole – dispense with any of its powers or parts.

This plainly metaphorical conception leads on, however, in Paul's thought to a more mystical one. Christians are exhorted, "have this mind in you which was also in Christ Jesus"; and to remember that "Christ is in you, by the Spirit that dwelleth in you"; and so to yield their members as instruments of righteousness unto God, and present their bodies as living sacrifices unto Him.

Here, the body of Jesus, maimed and torn upon the cross, has been replaced by one whose members are the limbs, tongues, eyes and hands, hearts and heads of an ever larger circle of devoted men and women; through whom the same truth, the same healing grace and transforming power, that men once met in Christ, still flow.

Later still in Paul's writings, the idea develops in a somewhat complicated and inconsistent way (as Paul's metaphors are liable to do!). Then the Church is seen as the Body, of which Christ is, not the indwelling life simply, but also the ascended Head, "from whom the whole body, joined and knit together by every joint with which it is supplied, when each part is working properly, makes bodily growth and upbuilds itself in love."

Seeing the Church thus, as in a restricted sense an "incarnation" or embodiment of the living Spirit of Jesus, still abroad in the earth and still seeking and saving that which is lost, Paul desired deeply to share that corporate indwelling of Christ. He refused to remain in impoverished isolation from all Christ's other "members". So, he endeavoured to join the disciples at Jerusalem: it is a valid reason still for uniting formally and loyally with the existing Church of Christ.

The School

A second clue to Paul's insistence at Jerusalem is offered in the idea, which occurs some thirty times in his writings, of the Christian's need to be "edified", to be "upbuilt" in faith, in character, and in usefulness. Many practical issues of Christian conduct – Church order, and worship, the observance or ignoring of holy days, eating or abstaining from meats previously offered in idol temples, the use of wine, and similar detailed controversial questions of personal ethic — are discussed by Paul in the light of the education of th young convert for life in pagan society. No binding laws, o universal rules, are established: but love and the edificatio of one's fellow Christian are the inescapable obligations.

Immense emphasis is laid upon the process of mutua teaching, counsel, exhortation, encouragement, rebuke, whicl in Paul's eyes was a primary function and chief value o Church life. The Church was to him a "school", of conduc and faith, of saintly living and effective service, of praye and worship. He thought of its fellowship as affordin inspiration for the fainthearted, example, counsel, and warn ing that could discipline young souls to maturity of faith an balanced completeness of character.

Paul knew and confessed his own need to learn *with al the saints* the full dimensions of Christ's love that canno be entirely explored within the limits of one life-experience We must all attain to the unity of the faith, to mature man hood, to the measure of the stature of the fulness of Christ — and Paul insists we cannot attain that high ideal alone.

It is not hard to discover where Paul might have learned thi practical conception of the value of the Church to developin Christian life. The Jewish synagogue had everywhere becom a school of Judaism, with formal catechism and an order o teaching-elders to expound and foster the Jewish faith. Th Scribes, too, were dedicated to the careful teaching o the Law, often for no reward but with great diligenc and learning.

Paul himself, like Theophilus (to whom Luke wrote) Apollos, and the Galatian converts, and indeed all whom the apostolic Church baptised, had been instructed ("cate chised") by Christian teachers set apart for that ministry And Paul would see no reason why the "education" of the soul should cease. The living community of Christians worshipping and serving in one place, was the best of all instructors in the life of God's kingdom: it was the school where men "learn Christ". And Paul, knowing his heart's need, demanded admittance.

The Pressure-Group

Paul certainly believed that the Church was God's chosen instrument for world redemption. He came to argue later, with great persuasiveness, that she was the successor in God's purposes to the family, the nation, the remnant, of Old Testament prophecy. God had ever chosen to work through an agent-community: the family of Abraham became the twelve clans of Israel, and later the nation called to worship and to witness for a sign among all peoples. The nation failing, God promised a remnant should survive to inherit the promises and fulfil the purposes of the ancient covenant with Israel. The remnant, too, proving faithless and ineffectual, God promised One, His Servant, who should do representatively the work for which Israel had been destined.

And Jesus gathered about Him the disciple band, earnest of His Church, the New Israel, and God's new agent-community. Paul was well aware of this divine principle of the pressure-group of elect and spiritually qualified individuals called to fulfil God's purpose in the earth. He saw the Church as God's agency in this dispensation, the means by which He would make known, now and in all the ages to come, His manifold wisdom as revealed in His kindness toward us in Christ Jesus. So Paul wrote to the Ephesians, but the idea that the Church is the focal point of divine activity among men is everywhere in his correspondence. It was in and through the Christian community in each place that the divine purpose and power invaded human society, entered history, touched human life with creative and enduring effect.

In consequence, the Church and its local life was the appointed avenue for service of God's cause. Paul could be no passenger Christian, and allowed none other to contract out of the ongoing work of the kingdom. His nature was too ardent and practical to be content with spiritual idleness: to be Christ's at all was to be Christ's servant. But equally, his mind was too realistic, too well-schooled in scriptural insights, to imagine that one voice, one soul, one private-enterprise isolationist in the field of the kingdom, could make much impact on a lost world. We are, and must be, workers together.

The widest, noisiest impression that any one individual makes in religious work is nothing compared with the steady influence of persistent, consecrated witness, through the years, woven into the life of a local community by a worthy and happy Christian fellowship. Paul's whole background, training, and apostolic experience confirmed this valuation of united, disciplined, spiritual team-work — and in any case it was God's will.

And so he wanted to join the Church because he wanted to count for Christ. That is a third valid reason, even yet, for submerging one's personal dedication and effort in the multiplied, co-ordinated consecration of some local fellowship of God's servants.

The Family

But if Paul's later words reveal his reasons for seeking membership at Jerusalem, we must add a fourth, more intimate argument. From all his attitude and exhortation in the following years, we know that Paul wanted the Church around him in times of adversity and stress.

It may well be that already he had seen something of the solidarity of Christians under persecution. He probably knew of the spontaneous generosity that knit the early Christians together, rich with poor, and of the warmth of fellowship and goodwill that marked their private meetings. Soon he was to learn from the inside how real that fellowship was, and his repeated thanksgivings for the enriching comradeship of brethren in Christ cannot be too often remarked.

The letter to Philippi breathes a warmth of affection and mutual trust that is still moving. The note to Philemon is a gem of Christian brotherliness. The second letter to Corinth reveals, as much by its references to the distress Paul had felt at the breach which had occurred, as by his joy over its healing, how very much the Corinthians' loyalty meant to Paul's heart. His sternness toward John Mark, who let him down, and towards all attitudes within the Church that destroyed mutual confidence, show from the other side how Paul valued Christian friendship.

The story of his commissioning by the Church at Antioch for his first missionary adventuring; the anticipation of "mutual refreshment" on his visit to Rome; the tender leave-taking of the elders at Miletus, as he faces his dangerous journey to Jerusalem; the repeated, urgent calls for prayer on his behalf; the beautiful story of his landing in Italy, and the deep encouragement and thanksgiving that mark his meeting with those who came to comfort him; the regretful admission that at his answer before Caesar "no man stood with me" — all such details of his story bear eloquent, because accidental, testimony to the exceptionally vivid sense of Christian comradeship by which Paul was sustained, and which he so much prized.

Paul needed, no less than we do, the fellowship of Christians around him in anxiety and disappointment, in temptation and danger, in labour and in sorrow. The Christian who pretends he does not need his brethren is nursing the foolish pride that goes before a serious fall. God who knows that it is never good for man to be alone, and who sets the solitary in families, sets Christians also in Churches, for their mutual good. That is a fourth sound reason, even yet, why individual Christians, who know their business and their own hearts, insist on joining the Church of Christ.

The Lord's Intention

Nevertheless, true though these assessments of the Church's purpose are to the mature thought of Paul, it would be wrong to suggest that merely utilitarian, self-centred reasons prompted Paul's conviction that conversion leads inevitably to Church membership. The matter went deeper than his own spiritual needs and their fulfilment through Christian fellowship. The unity of all believers in the Church of the living God was a necessary implication of the gospel itself, and membership could not be left to personal inclination or need.

Paul was convinced that the Church held foremost place in the intention of Jesus. He declared, "Christ loved the Church and gave himself up for her, that he might sanctify her, having cleansed her by the washing of water with the word, that the Church might be presented before him in splendour, without spot or wrinkle or any such thing, that she might be holy and without blemish . . . He nourishes and cherishes it . . . Christ is himself its Saviour." The Church is "his glorious inheritance in the saints", and "obtained with his own blood". As in one metaphor Christ is its Head, so in another He is the one foundation, already laid, which none dare change.

In this light, Paul traces all that is important to the Church's life back to the will of Christ. Her ministers — apostles, prophets, pastors, teachers, and the rest — are gifts to the Church by the ascended Lord. The various talents manifested usefully in the Church's life are gifts of the Holy Spirit for the Church's edification. The Church's worship moves around the two focal occasions, baptism and the Lord's Supper. In the former, "by one Spirit we were all baptised into one body", "were baptised into Christ". And the Lord's Table, likewise, is set within the Church with the authority of Christ's treasured command, for an act of shared remembrance: it was "received of the Lord", and it was He who said, "Do this . . . Do this . . ."

The individualist Christian, therefore, sitting lightly to all Church loyalties, and tempted sometimes to depreciate "organised Christianity", must expect no sympathy from Paul. The Church was Christ's intention. It was also, as we have seen, a spiritual necessity. And Paul might have added (if his mind had worked in such a way) that it was a logical consequence of Christ. For Christ's ideal is the kingdom, which necessitates a society, a community, of hearts obedient to God; Christ's demand is service, which necessitates recognition of others' need and co-operation in meeting it; and Christ's law is love — which no man can fulfil alone. If Paul does not in fact express these truths in quite these terms, he is certainly aware of their force, and urges their substance upon each of his Churches.

Of all Christ's followers, Paul might with greatest reason have supposed that he could afford to pursue his Christian life without too great concern for the joys and sorrows, the obligations and disciplines, the detailed duties and domestic tensions of local Church life. In fact, he is no sooner a Christian than he is in the deepest sense a Churchman. That is very significant, and deeply instructive.

PAUL THE CHRISTIAN

His Certainties: "We Know . . ."

His Centralities: "In Christ"

His Character: "The Gentleness of Christ"

His Consecration: "To Me To Live Is Christ"

His Companions: "My Fellow Workers"

His Citizenship: "I Appeal to Caesar"

8 *His Certainties: "We Know . . ."*

THE WORKING CREED of Paul the Christian may conveniently be gathered from his repeated affirmations in the form "We know . . ." It is true that a full statement of Paul's faith would include many further declarations, of a more theological kind, and numerous firm and clear judgements on questions of belief and principle that we do well to treasure and to heed. Yet the basic and controlling beliefs of any career are comparatively few. The more firmly they are held, the fewer they are.

We set upon one side mere religious opinions, more or less soundly based upon knowledge and insight, but liable to be changed with wider experience and fuller understanding. We set upon the other side things believed upon another's authority, as the best available explanations of difficult questions, or the consensus of opinion among those who should know, but always accepted with certain mental reservations and held with due humility. What remains are personal convictions, proved in experience, built upon as unshakably true for us, claiming allegiance at any cost, to be held "though the heavens fall". These fundamental beliefs cannot be many, but they are enormously powerful. They predestinate the life, they shape the character – indeed, they *are* the man.

In Paul's case we may assume, as matter of obvious fact, the existence, sovereignty, goodness, and nearness of God. In Paul's world only fools would doubt it, and they were few, and negligible. As surely as the sun shone, as surely as the seasons moved in procession, as surely as the miracle of birth and the mystery of death continued, as surely as the Law and the prophets spoke to the human conscience, as surely as the whole Hebrew revelation was written in the Jewish character and State, so surely did God, the Creator and King, Judge and Redeemer, sit enthroned in heaven. Paul would as little think of doubting that as questioning the earth beneath his feet, or the fact of his own existence. From that premise all his religion started; upon the divine Fact all his life was built; to the fulfilment of God's purposes, as he understood them, all his days were consciously directed. Though his conversion to Christ brought him a better understanding, it could not convey to him a deeper certainty concerning God. But four other certainties Christ did impart, the first a sombre conviction about himself.

Sin

Remembering Paul's long struggle and deepening disillusion, we should not be surprised to hear him say, "I know that nothing good dwells within me, that is, in my flesh." Nor should we dismiss the melancholy confession as a passing pessimism, – and certainly not as a mere exaggeration of modesty. The conviction is fundamental to all Paul's Christian consciousness.

In frail and fallen human nature resides no fount of creative goodness. Paul had trodden the dark valley of humiliating self-knowledge before that realisation possessed his mind. All that he says of grace, and divine election, of the power of the gospel and the utter necessity of Christ, rests upon this unqualified admission of human bankruptcy. The human problem is too great for human resolution just because the human problem is – Man. Man, sin, and death are humanity's worst enemies, and God the only Friend. Only that last confidence saves Paul's anthropology from unrelieved despair.

In one strong, ambiguous phrase Paul speaks of the mystery of iniquity, and whatever else he meant, he certainly included what we now call the "demonic" element in evil. For evil *is* a mystery: its very presence in God's world, as lies, greed, lust, hate, selfishness, cruelty and folly, is mysterious. So is its strange, pervasive power to fascinate, enslave, deceive, degrade, and finally destroy, to contaminate innocence, corrupt civilisations, and menace the whole world.

Mysterious, too, is its persistence, poisoning the very springs of life, passing on through generations to overshadow even the unborn, reaping its dread harvest in each new age as the entailed heritage of the race, from which none can escape. No responsible analysis of man's predicament denies this alien force in human society, this universal factor of the love of wrong, to be reckoned with in all schemes for human betterment. Whatever the explanations offered – evolution, the racial sub-conscious, ignorance, or what else – the fact confronts us.

Paul sets beside this mystery of evil, the mystery of godliness — its presence in such a world, rising in heroic figures to challenge and outlive each dark age; its power to win, redeem, cleanse and restore, and recreate hope and courage; and its persistence in spite of adversity, temptation, apparent defeat and seeming despair. This is the dilemma of human thought: if this is a good world, we are baffled by the mystery of evil within it; if we despair and condemn it as an evil world, we are moved and confounded by the sheer goodness it enshrines! And crowning the mystery of godliness, for Paul and for all who share his faith, is the mystery of Christ — His presence in history, His power in human experience, His persistence in the ongoing life of the world. For He, too, is inexplicable — without God.

And so the realistic acknowledgement of the fact of evil bred in Paul no abject, self-pitying pessimism, no pseudo-clever cynicism. He faces it frankly, because he knows he has discovered its solution. He has little interest in theoretic explanations. Sometimes he seems to trace human sinfulness to the sin of Adam, though more as illustration than as origin. Sometimes he speaks of the presence in the world of demon-powers, alien forces antagonistic to God, which work man's spiritual undoing and slavery — but he never doubts that man remains responsible for his own wrong-doing. Sometimes he speaks rather as though sin itself were a power within man's sensual nature, dividing the personality from within, and too often enslaving the higher powers through weakness of will.

But historical, demonic, or psychological explanations apart, Paul is certain of the fact of sin. He has taken its measure, he reckons with its power. Like his Master, Paul is essentially a realist, and so insured against much disappointment and doubt; in that undespairing realism lies maturity of faith. It is part of Paul's practical outlook, both as Christian and as apostle, to know that within man himself dwells no power of good: man needs a Saviour.

Christ

But Paul's second certainty is that man has found one. "I know," he declares, "whom I have believed and I am sure that he is able to guard until that Day what has been entrusted to me" (or, as the margin's version suggests, "what I have entrusted to him"). This is the certainty concerning Christ which only personal relationship can establish. Through a long, and infinitely changeful, career of travel and adventure, toil and hardship, persecution and peril, and great achievement, Paul had learned in experience the peerless character, the purposeful will, the sufficient power, the perfect sympathy, of the Saviour Christ.

Paul had discovered by personal experiment how entirely true was the Master's word, how faithful His promise, how dependable His present aid, how adequate His example and His counsel, how precious His companionship. He had been able to save – even Paul of Tarsus! He had proved able to keep, even amid great pressures and perils. He would prove able to guard until that Day. Christ was worthy of all trust: that was unquestionably one of Paul's bedrock certainties.

But there is something more Paul would say. He has implicit, and unbounded, confidence in Christ – has he similar confidence in his own faithfulness? Is he sure that he will never lose faith, or fall away? Paul's answer must be gleaned from a glowing passage that has been treasured wherever the New Testament has been read: the tonic, bracing, sweeping paragraph at the end of chapter eight in his letter to Rome. Contemplating the fulness and sufficiency of God's plan for man's salvation, Paul suddenly breaks out – "What then shall we say to this?" For once the eloquent apostle is left speechless!

Yet he finds great things to say. One is, that if the almighty God is *for us,* on our side, then he who opposes matters nothing, whoever he might be. That God *is* for us, is almost the heart of the gospel: it is the very meaning of reconciliation, it is the obvious implication of God's loving us at all, it is the reason why Christ came, it is the experience of believing hearts. He is for us, all the time, in all circumstances, all through the years, to succour, to save, to sanctify, to outmatch every adversary. For God in Christ has become our covenant-Redeemer.

And God provides for us, *all* things. Peter, more cautiously, says "all things that pertain to life and godliness", but Paul will acknowledge no limitation to the divine generosity. Three times his superabounding confidence rings out: *all things* that make up experience work; in *all things* that threaten the soul we are more than conquerors; *all things* that are needful are freely given. All that the Christian soul endures, or fears, or hungers for, is explicitly guaranteed; for "He who did not spare His own Son, but gave him up for us all, will he not also give us all things with him?" We are people of little expectation and small prayers, of nervous asking and timorous taking, because we do not, like Paul, measure the divine generosity by the cross.

Once again, God fights for us, in all assaults of our enemies. "Who shall bring any charge against God's elect?" Envious, slanderous men may do so; conscience may. But "it is God who justifies" – and all accusation is silenced. "Who is to condemn?" The world might; God could have done so. But Christ Jesus died, was raised again, and intercedes for us at the right hand of God, that condemnation might be removed from us. Then "Who shall separate us from the love of Christ?" Shall tribulation, distress, persecution, famine, nakedness, peril, sword? Shall death or life, angelic principalities and powers, things present or things to come? No! All are provided against. He who so planned, and has performed salvation, will perfect it until the Day of Christ. God will see us through.

That is Paul's answer. Nothing shall sever us from Him. His hold, not ours, is the strength of our security; His faithfulness, not ours, is the basis of our hope; His patience, not ours, is the foundation of our perseverance; His defence, not ours, the guarantee that we need never fall away, shall never be separated from the love of God in Christ Jesus our Lord.

The Christian is strong, because God is for us; he is satisfied, because God provides for us; he is safe, because God defends us. Succour, sufficiency, security are pledged to us in Christ – and we know whom we have believed! On that tested certainty Paul built his whole career.

Providence

This stirring declaration of sublime confidence in Christ has already recalled the strong words of Paul affirming that God's over-ruling providence shapes all experience to divine ends. In a passage full of vicissitude and peril, of hunger and nakedness, of sighs and searched hearts, of accusation and distress, of persecution and the fear of death – and fear of life – Paul can still declare, "*We know* that in everything God works for good with those who love him, who are called according to his purpose . . ."

It is always important to remember here that the purpose God has in view is clearly defined in Paul's next sentence. We are "predestined to be conformed to the image of his Son"; that is the great end towards which the Christian's daily experience is divinely patterned. It is important, too, to note the limitation of the principle to those who love God, and who therefore accept His purpose for their lives, and surrender confidently to the pattern He imposes on their experience. To rebel against His will for want of trust, or in resentful self-pity, is to frustrate the gracious purpose God has in view. For such lives, all things do not work together, nor work for good.

But given faith, and obedience, nothing that happens in our lives is wasted: "all things work"; nothing that happens must be evaluated by itself, for "all things work together"; and nothing that happens can occasion ultimate harm, for "all things work together for good." For God is good. That is a stabilising faith with which to face adversity.

To the Christian, "all things are of God"; and Paul can assert the consequence of this: "All things are yours, whether Paul or Apollos or Cephas or the world or life or death or the present or the future, all are yours and you are Christ's and Christ is God's." Written to a Church despised, few, impoverished and threatened, these were bold words, yet so sure is Paul of the over-ruling hand of God, and the unswerving purpose that subjects all experience to spiritual ends, that he declares – in opposition to the narrow, fearful, timid spirit that looks on life with suspicion and dread – All things are for our enrichment, whatsoever things are true, honest, just, pure, lovely, of good report, so "Think on these things".

And all things are for our acceptance. Differing spiritual leaders (like Paul, and Apollos, and Cephas), differing meats and customs and traditions (like Gentile and Jewish viewpoints in one Church), all can contribute to the total treasure of spiritual life. All things are for our sakes – even imprisonment can work out for the furtherance of the gospel, and suffering produces endurance, endurance produces character, and character produces hope. To the faithful heart nothing comes amiss. And yet again, all things are available for our need: "My God shall supply every need of yours . . . God is able to provide you with every blessing in abundance, so that you may always have enough of everything, and may provide in abundance for every good work."

Such is Paul's confidence in the divine direction and care. Life with all its challenge and opportunity, death with all its mystery and grief, things present with their demands, confusions and needs, things to come with all their mingled hope and menace – all are ours, to serve our need, be subject to our good, as we are Christ's. In that confidence Paul could travel, work, suffer or die, unafraid, committing himself and all his affairs to a sovereign hand that made all experience contribute, somehow, but surely, to ultimate good.

Immortality

The fateful insufficiency of human resources, the entire sufficiency of Christ, the all-sufficiency of God's over-ruling providence – Paul's basic Christian assumptions – are crowned and completed by an ever-sufficient hope: "We know," he cries, "that if the earthly tent we live in is destroyed, we have a building from God, a house not made with hands, eternal in the heavens."

Behind this conviction lay the memory of the vision of the ascended Lord, and a long life of fellowship with the risen One, establishing once and for all the vague hope of immortality which Paul first learned as a Pharisee. Now that hope, consolidated into certainty, irradiated all his work. His labour was pursued in the knowledge that "the Day" would expose any worthless materials, any slovenly workmanship. He advised on marriage, on slavery, on conduct in general, in the light of the brevity of time left before the Advent and everlasting life.

Paul saw in Christ "the hope of glory"; he entrusted his soul to Jesus "against that Day"; he awaited a Saviour from heaven who would change our lowly body to be like His glorious body; he believed that when "Christ who is our life appears, then you also will appear with him in glory." He longs to be "with Christ, for that is far better". And not Christians only, but the whole "creation waits with eager longing for the revealing of the sons of God . . . the redemption of our bodies," and that divine end, when Christ delivers the kingdom to God the Father, having conquered death itself, and "God may be everything to everyone."

All this is plainly near to the nerve of Paul's working faith. It is no mere appendage to other beliefs, no logical deduction from the general tenor of religion: it is interwoven with all his thought of Christ, and an abiding inspiration for his daily life. All his experience is enriched by the hope of immortality; all his decisions are made more significant by their eternal consequences; all struggle is made worthwhile for its infinite reward. Love is more enriching for its unbreakable endurance; duty is more demanding for its timeless authority; sacrifice, injustice, suffering are made more tolerable for their certain vindication.

To believe in immortality was not, for Paul, an escapist trap-door into a world of wishful ease, but the inexhaustible stimulus to nobler living and more strenuous toil. The end of all his argument about the resurrection of Jesus is immensely practical: "Therefore, my beloved brethren, be steadfast, immovable, always abounding in the work of the Lord, knowing that in the Lord your labour is not in vain."

Such in Paul's view are the cornerstone certainties of Christian faith: sin, Christ, providence and everlasting life. Possessing these, and being possessed by them, a man will build the house of his life foursquare to every blast, and know that in the storm his house will stand.

9 *His Centralities: "In Christ"*

THE CENTRE of life appears, with Paul, to be somewhat crowded. Several conceptions might fairly be called "central" to his thinking: the cross, the resurrection of Jesus, the Spirit, the imitation of Christ, are examples. Several others, as the divine righteousness, the sacrificial system, God's covenant with Israel and so with the Church, might be considered central to his doctrinal pattern. If we were interested mainly in his spiritual development, or in his apostolic career, we should name other things as "central" – the Damascus Road and Roman citizenship, a pioneering spirit and loyal colleagues, Judaist training and a brilliant mind.

Yet behind all the separate aspects of Paul as thinker and teacher, apostle, evangelist and pastor, stands the man, the Christian – admittedly difficult to distinguish from the rest in a life so manifestly of one piece. It is worthwhile therefore to try to isolate the things which Paul, as an individual Christian, sought to keep central, amid all the manifold interests, pressures and distractions of his full life.

"Ye were called into the fellowship of [God's] Son, Jesus Christ our Lord." There, for Paul, was the focus of all centralities – the living companionship of the risen Christ. Highly as Paul valued the authentic gospel tradition concerning Jesus, and the informed faith built thereon, and though he shared to the full the worship and ordinances of the Church, and insisted upon the moral obligations of Christian discipleship, yet for him the essence of Christianity was neither knowledge, Church loyalty, nor ethics, but life in closest union with his living Lord.

So Christian life had begun for him, in personal encounter with Christ. So it continued, in personal experience of Christ's living presence through every day: "the Lord is near". And so he confidently hoped it would end, departing to be "with Christ, for that is far better".

Nearly two hundred and forty times Paul uses, as a kind of shorthand phrase for all that being a Christian implied, the words "in Christ", or "in the Lord". This expression is almost Paul's definition of Christianity: as H. R. Mackintosh says, "Around this idea his religious feeling crystallised . . . It is used with reference to every side of experience; 'I am persuaded in Christ . . . If there be any consolation in Christ . . . The dead in Christ . . .' "

To illustrate the meaning of Paul's thought, "Christ in us, we in Christ", it is usual to compare Christ to "the Christian's native air" – at once within a man as breath, essential to his life, and yet outside him as "atmosphere", the necessary environment in which he lives. As fish live "in" the only element in which they can survive, as birds live "within" the air that carries them, as branches live only so long as they remain "within" the living plant, and limbs only so long as they remain within the wholeness of the living body, so the Christian lives "in Christ", at once his life, his breath, his spiritual environment, the necessary background and basis of his very existence.

A relationship so essential must be continuous, yet at certain moments even Paul felt its reality and power with exceptional vividness. Arrested and imprisoned at Jerusalem, himself the storm-centre of a bitter controversy that might well issue in death, Paul lay in some dejection in the Roman barracks above the Temple: but "the Lord stood by him, and said . . . Take courage."

On board ship, a prisoner still, bound for Rome and Caesar's court but meanwhile storm-beaten and likely to shipwreck, Paul could still say, "This very night there stood by me an angel of the God to whom I belong and whom I worship and he said, 'Do not be afraid'." And later still, of his appearance in Caesar's judgement hall, he could say, "At my first defence no one took my part . . . But the Lord stood by me and gave me strength . . ." Nevertheless, these are only the recorded high-lights of an experience whose characteristic quality was the enjoyment from day to day, unbrokenly, of the fellowship of God's Son.

We may say, if we so choose, that this "mystical" language is only a vigorous metaphor for faith in Christ – provided we remember always that faith has for Paul this deeper meaning of personal relationship, and must not be reduced to mere belief, or even to simple trust. One of Paul's most revealing words about his inner life lends emphasis to this: I live, he says, by faith in the Son of God. The point is important: the relationship expressed in the phrase "in Christ" needed, for its maintenance, the watchful exercise and re-affirmation of continued faith, if it was not to become yet another empty form of words.

We must say (because Paul said it) that such relationship to Christ involves identification with Him in His suffering, death, and resurrection, as Christian baptism so dramatically sets forth. This, too, is important, because another exercise necessary to remaining "in Christ" is the constant reckoning oneself dead indeed unto sin but alive unto God through Him.

We should say, thirdly, that life "in Christ" may well be described in terms of love, for Paul loved Christ with an ardent, eager, enjoying loyalty unexcelled in Christian history. To be in Christ was to be in love, and to remain in Christ required that Christ remain pre-eminent in all the soul's affection, obedience, and desire.

Even so, it is always impossible to analyse personal relationship entirely into its constituent elements – something is always lost in the process, and usually something warm, intimate and indefinable. Faith, identification with Christ, and love for Him are several aspects – but no more – of that one inclusive and enriching union of Paul with Christ which made of Christian life one long Emmaus walk with the risen Jesus, from outside Damascus to the everlasting Presence.

Prayer

It is at first sight unconvincing – too conventional to be strictly true – to say that Paul's inward fellowship with Christ was sustained and made articulate in a life of prayerfulness. Paul is so obviously a man of action, and of thought, that he seems barely comfortable among the Church's great exponents of the devotional life. Quiet contemplation and spiritual retreat appear foreign to his energetic nature, and the pensive cloister would have seemed to him a prison.

Yet Paul was first announced in Christian circles as a man given to prayer. The opening words of Christ to Ananias concerning him say precisely this: "Rise . . . Go . . . Enquire . . . for a man of Tarsus named Saul: for behold, he is praying." And so Paul continued. In letter after letter he is able to assure his Churches and correspondents of their place in his constant intercession: "in every prayer of mine for you all," to the Philippians; "I mention you always in my prayers," to the Romans; and similarly to the Ephesians, to the Thessalonians (adding "night and day"), to Timothy and Philemon. "We have not ceased to pray for you" he tells the Colossians.

This is more than evidence of epistolary politeness: it is the record of a pastoral ministry of prayer as wide as his physical travelling, as full as his noble heart. Sometimes Paul names the particular requests he makes: that the Corinthians will "do no wrong"; that the Philippians' love "may abound"; that the Thessalonians may be wholly sanctified, spirit, soul and body being kept sound and blameless at the coming of Christ. He records, too, his constant prayers for Israel.

Occasionally we are allowed glimpses of that life of prayer; of the fasting and prayer at Antioch as the first missionary couple set out, and again as the Churches of Galatia are consolidated and organised, on the return journey. The missionaries seek the place of prayer at Philippi – and soon are praying in prison, to considerable effect! When Paul for the last time takes leave of the elders of Ephesus at Miletus, a sorrowful season of prayer is held, and something very similar happened later at Tyre. At Malta Paul prays for the healing of Publius, chief of the island. It is this habit of prayerfulness, rather than the length of prayers, that marks a man of prayer, and opens a highway for God through all his life.

Almost equally significant, however, is a man's awareness of his dependence on the prayers of others. Philemon is told that Paul's hope of seeing him again depends upon Philemon's prayers. Paul tells the Corinthians, "You also must help us by prayer"; he urges the Thessalonians (twice), and also the Colossians, "Brethren, pray for us"; he pleads with the Romans, "I appeal to you, brethren, by our Lord Jesus Christ and by the love of the Spirit, to strive together with me in your prayers to God on my behalf . . ."; and he assures the Philippians that his imprisonment will end in deliverance "through your prayers and the help of the Spirit of Jesus Christ."

These are the willing admissions of a heart that understands well how much it needs the prayer of friends and colleagues, and longs, in hard-pressed moments, to know that others bear him up before God's throne.

For all this, no systematic or detailed counsel about prayer is found in Paul's correspondence with his Churches. Doubtless he gave more instruction about it orally, and he does urge constancy: "Pray constantly . . . continue steadfastly in prayer, being watchful in it . . . Pray at all times in the Spirit, with all prayer and supplication . . . To that end keep alert, with all perseverance . . . Be constant in prayer." He pleads, too, that prayer be intelligent: "I will pray with the spirit, and I will pray with the mind also" – a warning offered to a congregation which tended towards emotionalism.

And Paul advises that prayer should have wide horizons. "Have no anxiety about anything, but in everything by prayer and supplication with thanksgiving let your requests be made known unto God. And the peace of God . . . will keep your hearts." For the rest, it may well be that to Paul's mind, prayer is to be learned by practice, especially by praying together, rather than by precept.

The petitions that preface several of Paul's letters are probably slightly more formal compositions, though not for that reason any less sincere. They are models of what might loosely be called the higher levels of prayer, requests for advancement in maturity of experience and in knowledge of the things of Christ. He asks that the love which the Philippians already show may abound still more, but with knowledge and discernment, so that with all their zeal and warm devotion they may yet see clearly and approve that which is *most* excellent, and so remain pure and blameless for the Day of Christ. Thus their love will be no idle emotion, but filled with all the fruits of righteousness which come through Christ, to the glory and praise of God. A thoughtful and discerning petition for a warm-hearted people!

For the Colossians, somewhat bewildered by speculation, by subtle variations of the gospel, by "philosophy and empty deceit", Paul prays that they may be filled with knowledge – not of theories, but – of God's will, in all *spiritual* wisdom and understanding; so that they may be equipped to lead lives worthy of the Lord, fully pleasing to Him, and bearing fruit in every good work. That was so much more important than bearing fruit in every current speculation! So, they would increase in true knowledge, the knowledge of God. He asks, too, that they may be strengthened with all power, according to God's glorious might, for all endurance, and for patience, and for the experiencing of great joy.

For the Ephesians Paul (in his letter) prays twice. First, that the Father of glory may give them a spirit of wisdom and revelation in the knowledge of Himself, the eyes of their hearts being enlightened to understand fully the hope to which they have been called, the riches of Christ's glorious inheritance in the saints, and the immeasurable greatness of God's power in those who believe.

As though that were not a sufficient request, he asks later that the Ephesian Christians might be strengthened, through God's Spirit, with might in the inner man; and that Christ may dwell, through faith, in their hearts. Thus, rooted and grounded in love, they may have the ability to comprehend with all saints what is the breadth and length and height and depth of the love of Christ – thus knowing it in all its measureless dimensions, though indeed it passes knowledge!. So knowing, they might be filled with all the fulness of God.

That Paul prays in such terms, with so large petitions, so penetrating spiritual insight, so rich a faith in God's power to answer, reveals how often his own heart has visited the throne of grace, and how vital, and central, to his daily experience among the Churches the habit of prayer had become.

Love

The Christian life has to be lived, however, not only in "the heavenly places", in Christ and in prayer, but among men; and for this aspect of daily Christian discipleship Paul has one central priority – the law of love. Love is, for him, the supreme rule of Christ, pre-eminently necessary to Christian living because Jesus said so. It is the outward manifestation of the love of God shed abroad in the heart by the Holy Spirit.

Without love, speaking ecstatically "with tongues", preaching the gospel, knowing the truth, working miracles, exercising faith, showing charity towards the poor, and even martyrdom, "profit nothing". It is the "more excellent way": unless a man is treading it, he cannot be following Christ. Moreover it is – in one word – the fulfilling of the whole

Law: from the over-riding duty of love all other duties towards one's neighbour, both positive obligations to help him and negative obligations not to harm him, directly follow.

To love is to let the mind of Christ dwell in us. It is to refrain from selfishness and conceit. It is humbly to count others better than ourselves. It is to look not alone upon our own interests, but also on the interests of others so as to serve their need at whatever cost to ourselves. It is to do as Jesus did for us.

To love is to feel such concern for weaker brethren, and even for foolish ones, as to set limits to one's own liberty of conscience, lest they be led astray. Love demands of us kindness, an unashamed tender-heartedness, and willingness to forgive each other as freely as God in Christ forgave us. Love therefore necessarily puts an end to falsehood, anger, dishonesty; to corrupting conversation, to bitterness, to slander, and to every sort and degree of malice.

For love makes the Christian soul patient and gentle. It just cannot be jealous or boastful, arrogant or rude. It does not insist on its own way, and is not irritable, or resentful, when it fails to get it. Love cannot rejoice, even secretly, at failure or wrong in others; but it is genuinely delighted when others do well. It bears all things without bitterness; it believes all good without suspicion; it hopes continually for good success, without cynicism; it endures all hardship without fainting. It never fails.

Nor is love just an abstract standard of mutual attitudes, setting a high value upon good personal relationships. It is not just a positive, creative sociability that transforms human "contacts" into enriching experience. It is also an active and spontaneous quality of behaviour, that delights in doing concrete good.

Amid all his endless journeying, writing, preaching, suffering, Paul found time, energy, and initiative to organise thoroughly a sea-wide collection among his Gentile Churches around the Aegean to help practically and domestically the hungry Christians in Judea. Because this was the way, Paul argued, that Gentile Churches might show their understanding of the gospel, the depth and sincerity of their experience of grace, the reality of their salvation — by showing love.

He roundly condemns the intellectual pride and self-assertiveness, the social pride and greed, that disrupted the

Church at Corinth, not only because they produced unseemly behaviour and chaotic disunity, but also because they offended deeply against the love that should bind rich and poor, wise and unwise, in one fellowship of Christ. In the same spirit, Paul brushed impatiently aside petty and abstract arguments over detailed issues of behaviour – meat, drink, festivals – when he suspected that the contenders had forgotten the over-ruling duty of walking charitably together. And as with intellectual and social divisions, so with the intractable problem of slavery: he demanded that mutual relations of master and slave should be subject in all respects to the Christian law of loyalty and goodwill – the rule of love.

Paul demands, too, that those benefitting from the spiritual ministry of teachers and pastors should share generously with their leaders in all good things, although he himself combined hand-wearing manual work with his evangelistic labours at Corinth, in order not to burden the embryo Church with having to maintain the apostolic pioneers. He insists that at all times a community of need or of plenty, of sorrow and of joy, shall be preserved in the Church's common life: liberal hospitality, mutual sharing of burdens, hard daily work to finance generous benefaction, are explicitly required of the Pauline Churches. And Paul very warmly commends the liberality of Macedonian Christians in sharing what little they possessed with others who had still less.

The apostle prohibits very sternly any engagement in lawsuits between Christians, as alien to a brotherhood of love. He himself will either insist upon his Roman rights and obtain apology for ill-treatment, or he will quietly slip away that opposition may die down, as best shall serve the interests of new converts who must go on living in that place. But he will dauntlessly return to towns and cities where he had been in peril (as Iconium, Lystra) in order to consolidate, comfort, and instruct the young Christians there.

Paul grieves personally for those who, like the Galatians, prove unstable. He enters feelingly into the anxieties of the Philippian Church about their beloved pastor's welfare, and about his own, and despite his own anxieties he writes understandingly to assure them. Moreover – shrewd test of a truly generous spirit – Paul knows how to accept the gifts of others with the gracious appreciation of a truly humble and grateful heart.

Love clearly meant for Paul not only an ethical principle of supreme and definitive importance in Christian moral teaching, but a daily discipline and endeavour that regulated all contacts with fellow-Christians and with the world by the spirit of Jesus. To him, that, again, was central to Christian living.

To live "in Christ", to persevere in prayer, to walk in love, may seem very ordinary, and simple, principles of every-day Christianity to distinguish as the centralities of Paul's discipleship. Of their far-ranging effectiveness, there can be no doubt. Of their close inter-relation, little need be said: only a heart living in Christ would continue in prayer, or sustain such love; only a heart constant in prayer would so live in Christ, and for men; only a heart vigilant in love could maintain such prayerfulness, or endure fellowship with the loving Christ. As for their simplicity – that is the surest hall-mark of their truth.

10 *His Character: "The Gentleness of Christ"*

By a curious injustice, not unfamiliar in Christian biography, honour can become the occasion of dislike, and fame arouse a popular aversion. Sometimes the exceptional skill, or strength, or achievement, with which a man becomes identified so obscures his real personality that those who are most ready to acknowledge his importance may yet find it hard to admire or love him. The apostle Paul suffers more than most from this distortion of his true image by the dimensions of his work.

For Paul stands in Christian history as a formidable figure. Probably the most popular image of him is that of the controversialist, delighting in the cut and thrust of theological debate, in logic barbed too often with invective, and sometimes failing in patience toward lesser souls.

It is quite exceptionally difficult to correct this impression of the apostle, although it is quite exceptionally unfair. To say, as should be said, that to those ardent contendings for theological principles we owe much of our modern understanding of Jesus' message; that his forcefulness of character won the allegiance of scores of helpers; that no mere self-seeker, using the forms of Christian service to fulfil driving ambitions within his own nature, could have achieved so much for the kingdom of God – all this, though true, does not make Paul any more attractive to those who marvel, but do not like him.

Perhaps the great ones of history, the far-seeing, profound, and courageous souls, could not easily be at the same time dominant personalities and charming social acquaintances. Yet it is bare justice to remember that it was Paul, the ruthless, dauntless, driving pioneer, who wrote the world's loveliest hymn to Christian love – a poem exquisitely matching form, language, and rhythms to its exalted subject-matter, and at the same time a theological (and psychological) argument of profound insight and appeal. This can be no accident, no freak of mind: it reveals a sensitive imagination, a loving spirit, a kinship with the Christ whom he (perhaps unconsciously) describes, that says much for Paul's own quality. So does his emphasis upon the gentler virtues as the characteristic "fruit of the Spirit" – love, joy, peace, patience, kindness, goodness, faithfulness, and gentleness.

The immensity of Paul's pastoral problem may be felt in the sharp contrast, in one passage, between stern warnings against falsehood, stealing, corrupting conversation, bitterness, wrath, anger, clamour and slander, and the suddenly moving appeal: "Be kind to one another, tender-hearted . . . Be imitators of God, as beloved children, and walk in love as Christ loved us . . ." Immature, and inexperienced, young converts finding their way in a pagan society needed every bracing, stimulating influence Paul could wield to keep their conscience keen and their ideals high. His sternness would be their strength. Yet there was need also for encouragement, and tender understanding, to forgive the erring, save the weak, rekindle hope and faith in the despairing.

Paul possessed such patience. "To the Jews I became as a Jew . . . to those outside the law . . . as one outside the law; to the weak I became weak . . . I have become all things to all men, that I might by all means save some . . . Who is weak, and I am not weak? Who is made to fall, and I am not indignant?" It is mistaken to talk of "reconciling" this aspect of Paul's character with his fiercer writing in the letters to Galatia and to Corinth. For all this strong controversy is motivated by pastoral – and even paternal – concern.

They are "foolish" Galatians, but it is the anguished reproach of one who also says, "Brethren, I beseech you . . . Have I then become your enemy by telling you the truth? My little children, with whom I am again in travail . . . I am perplexed about you . . . Who has bewitched you?" The anger is for "those who unsettle you . . . and want to pervert the gospel of Christ", and it is justified; for the issue at stake was not personal prestige, or a debating victory, but the spiritual assurance of young converts that the gospel they had believed was divine truth, and the vindication in Christ's name of the whole Gentile mission policy.

In the correspondence with Corinth this blend of forcefulness and tenderness is especially evident, as Paul contends for his vision of Christian morality and love against the compromises, sins, and divisions of a particularly unstable Church. Here his sternness appears at its most formidable;

there is much of argument, rebuke, expostulation; and in respect of a flagrant breach of sexual morality within the Church, there is clear instruction that the offender "be removed from among you". There is also a most solemn pronouncing of judgement in the name of the Lord Jesus, and this is to be formally re-affirmed by the Church, assembled when "my spirit is present, with the power of our Lord Jesus" to deliver the sinning man "to Satan for the destruction of the flesh, that his spirit may be saved in the day of the Lord Jesus." The dreadful indictment ends: "Drive out the wicked person from among you."

Here again the prevailing vice of Corinthian society must be remembered, and the danger for Christianity itself if open incest be permitted unrebuked within the Church's fellowship. It is merely silly to suggest that Paul should have been more patient in these circumstances. But what astonishes beyond all expectation is his ready forgiveness of the man, and his own ratification of the Church's merciful dealing with him, when the sternness has done its necessary work. "If anyone has caused pain, he has caused it not to me but in some measure – not to put it too severely – to you all. For such a one this punishment by the majority is enough: so you should rather turn to forgive and comfort him, or he may be overwhelmed by excessive sorrow. So I beg you to re-affirm your love for him . . . Any one whom you forgive, I also forgive . . ."

Yet this should not astonish us. Sympathy, appeal, winsomeness, are mingled with all the serious warnings and firmer exhortations that Paul addresses to this Church. "Our mouth is open to you, Corinthians, our heart is wide . . . In return – I speak as to children – widen your hearts also . . . open your hearts to us . . . You are in our hearts, to die together and to live together. I have great confidence in you; I have great pride in you . . ." And again, "I, Paul, myself entreat you, by the meekness and gentleness of Christ . . . I beg of you that when I am present I may not have to show boldness . . . Do bear with me! I feel a divine jealousy for you, for I betrothed you to Christ. I did not burden anyone . . . And why, Because I do not love you? God knows I do!" The whole spirit of his faithful pastoral relationship with this Church is condensed in one other sentence: "It is in the sight of God that we have been speaking in Christ, and all for your upbuilding, beloved."

In this light we can appreciate the immense relief Paul felt when the tensions were over and all was well again. Then he could recall how he had written "out of much affliction and anguish of heart and with many tears, not to cause you pain but to let you know the abundant love that I have for you."

It has been said that Paul was essentially "a man of heart; he could love, and he had the power of compelling love . . . It is astonishing how often he is seen in tears . . ." The scene at Miletus, when the elders of Ephesus "all wept and embraced Paul and kissed him, sorrowing most of all because of the word he had spoken, that they should see his face no more", is typical of his personal relationships. The intimate note to Philemon breathes the very essence of close Christian friendship, and similar tones of affectionate interest mark most of the personal references at the close of his epistles. Writing to Timothy and to Titus, the apostle is concerned with details of their health, timidity, discouragement, anxious to safeguard from pitfalls of heresy and of pride, and eager at all points to strengthen their hands with the assurance of his authority and friendship.

Sternness and patience are the dual marks of Paul's dealing with another young colleague. There is a quality of ruthlessness in Paul's refusal to take John Mark on the second missionary journey because earlier Mark had "withdrawn . . . and had not gone with them to the work." But Mark is not abandoned: he goes with Barnabas, and the combined effect of Paul's sternness and Barnabas' support is to teach Mark new devotion, as Paul himself later handsomely acknowledges.

Paul's quick sympathy is nowhere better shown than in his discussion of relations between the "strong", whose informed and mature consciences find their way robustly among delicate issues of minor Christian morality (meats, drinks, holy days), and the "weak", who, unsure of themselves and of their principles, eschew all liberties and bind themselves by strictest codes of abstinence and separation. Paul argues for the "strong" position – but adds, it is the conscience of the weak that the strong must consider, and the effect of their example on the brother confused in mind and uneasy in heart. "Do not for the sake of food destroy the work of

God . . . It is right not to eat meat or drink wine or do anything that makes your brother stumble. We who are strong ought to bear with the failings of the weak and not to please ourselves."

There is a world of spiritual understanding in that voluntary abnegation of personal liberty for another's sake. But Paul is not done. As for what you may think of such weakness, "Who are you to pass judgement on the servant of another? It is before his own master that he stands or falls." Then the swift partisanship, stepping beside the weaker man in loving reassurance – "And he will be upheld, for the Master is able to make him stand." That enshrines the deep insight and extreme care of a very gentle heart.

On a different level, but of the same gentle quality, is his careful instruction and strong comforting of those at Thessalonica who had suffered bereavement, intensified by sore perplexity because it seemed those they had loved had missed the Christian hope of Christ's return. Paul patiently teaches a wiser, less excited, adventism; and then, turning to the sorrowing, with exquisite understanding and meticulous choice of words he penned a passage that, by its calm certainty, its appeal to the story and words of Jesus, its impressive imagery, its authority and tenderness, has brought unmeasured comfort "concerning those that are asleep" to generation after generation of Christian mourners.

"We were gentle among you, like a nurse taking care of her children." It would not occur to most of us to liken Paul to a prim and pretty nursemaid, engaged upon essentially feminine tasks: yet the Thessalonians would evidently see nothing incongruous in Paul's expression – though others might think the picture somewhat incomplete. For all that, enough has been said of Paul's sympathy with the troubled conscience and sorrowing heart to justify our contention that, behind the vigour of his mind and the force of his impact upon Christian history, there was that about him which fully entitled him to appeal "by the meekness and gentleness of Christ."

Courage

No one having the least acquaintance with Paul's long career of "great endurance in afflictions, hardships, calamities, beatings, imprisonments, tumults, labours, watching, hunger" can doubt the personal courage that formed the foundation of his personality. Paul cheerfully recites the story: "Five times . . . the forty lashes less one. Three times . . . beaten with rods; once stoned. Three times . . . shipwrecked; a night and a day . . . adrift at sea; on frequent journeys, in danger from rivers . . . from robbers . . . from my own people . . . from Gentiles . . . in the city . . . in the wilderness . . . at sea . . . from false brethren; in toil and hardship, through many a sleepless night, in hunger and thirst, often without food, in cold and exposure."

In the very listing of adversities one feels the untroubled confidence: "In all these things we are more than conquerors." And when the dangers lie not behind but ahead, the same courage hails them with defiance: "What are you doing, weeping and breaking my heart? For I am ready not only to be imprisoned but even to die . . . for the name of the Lord Jesus. I am going to Jerusalem, bound in the Spirit, not knowing what shall befall me there; except that the Holy Spirit testifies to me in every city that imprisonment and afflictions await me. But I do not account my life of any value nor as precious to myself, if only I may accomplish my course . . ."

"Once I was stoned": the simple phrase covers the narrow escape from tragedy at Lystra. "Jews came there from Antioch and Iconium; and having persuaded the people, they stoned Paul and dragged him out of the city, supposing that he was dead. But when the disciples gathered about him, he rose up and entered the city, and on the next day he went on . . ." In those final words the courage of Paul is perfectly expressed.

It needed little effort from such a man to keep his head, alone cool and practical, on a doomed ship; or to lie on his side, back bleeding, feet in the stocks, singing in prison.

And moral courage matched physical. The circumstances, and the cost, of his conversion show his fearless acceptance of truth once he had seen it. His clarity and firmness in situations that would make most men ready for compromise, eager to hold converts at almost any price of principle, shows spiritual leadership of the highest degree, open to misunderstanding and abuse, yet courageously right.

Paul will not cringe before Agrippa, but speaks the gospel boldly, asking no favours; arraigned before Felix, he pleads nothing, but rather attacks. For two years at Caesarea he maintains his case, refusing to descend to bribes, and at Philippi he will not leave in secret in the early morning when the magistrates grant him freedom, but for the sake of the Philippian converts demands a formal apology. At Ephesus he has to be restrained by friends from entering the theatre to address a rioting mob; and again at Jerusalem, bruised and bleeding, having barely escaped being torn in pieces, he persuades a Roman officer to let him face the crowd.

Nothing could frighten Paul's dauntless soul, nothing deflect his purpose, or intimidate his judgement. As the whole Christian cause of Church *versus* State moved to its climax of pressure and peril, the Church could have found no stauncher champion in whom the conflict might be focussed, or by whom the stedfastness and courage of all Christian hearts could be nourished and inspired.

Adversity

It is, however, in the handling of private adversity that character is most fiercely tested, and strength, or weakness, relentlessly exposed. Paul had to face from time to time rejection and affliction in several forms, and in each situation he manifested a rare humility of spirit.

All the indications are that Paul had been accustomed to considerable wealth: his pre-Christian career presupposes it, and his having learned a trade is no evidence to the contrary, for all Jewish lads were so taught. At Corinth he worked at his tent-making with Aquila and Priscilla, and the painful effects of this labour upon the hands may lend force to three references to his hands when recalling this earning of his own bread. "I coveted no one's silver or gold or apparel. You yourselves know that these hands ministered to my necessities, and to those who were with me . . . We labour, working with our own hands . . . You remember our labour and toil, brethren; we worked night and day, that we might not burden any of you . . . We were not idle . . . we did not eat any one's bread without paying . . ."

Yet Paul argues very strongly, from the Law, from the words of Jesus, and from the justice of the matter, that 'they who proclaim the gospel should get their living by the gospel", and often he accepted the gifts of the Churches to set him free to concentrate upon evangelism. In prison, and occasionally (as at Corinth) out of it, he was "in want", and work, gifts and want all argue the same conclusion: Paul possessed no private source of wealth. Among the lists of hardships borne, hunger figures five times, with cold and nakedness; "as having nothing . . . as poor" is part of his description of his constant situation. What this meant for his once-affluent spirit may be unconsciously revealed when he names as opposites of "plenty and abundance", "hunger, want, and *abasement*" – the last word hinting at the secret sense of humiliation, the inability to lift one's head in confidence in wealthy company, which only the poor man who has once been rich can really understand.

The breach with his family at conversion may explain Paul's poverty, and his words about "suffering the loss of all things" might well include the forfeiting of social and financial security for Christ's sake. It is impossible to be confident that Paul's offer to repay Philemon, and his dwelling in Rome in his own hired house, betray changed circumstances in later life: the gift of the Philippians belongs to the same period, in all probability. What is certain is that actual experience lies behind his testimony: "I have learned, in whatever state I am, to be content. I know how to be abased, and I know how to abound; in any and all circumstances I have learned the secret of facing plenty and hunger, abundance and want. I can do all things in him who strengthens me."

And behind this attitude again is the humble spirit that contends for no "rights" in such a matter, that demands no reward, that sees no reason why, in spite of all talents, toil, and training, it should not suffer want with Him who had not where to lay His head. There is about the words "I am initiated into the secret . . . to be content" a faint ring of self-satisfaction resembling that of the Stoic, but this is immediately corrected by the ascription of all success and strength to "him who enables me". It is still in acknowledged weakness that Paul finds his sufficiency.

Poverty is hard, but it is an equally bitter thing fo
an ardent and gifted man to suffer rejection by those h
desperately longs to serve; and wounded pride can sometime
feed upon that bitterness to nourish impatience and despair
Paul faced such rejection repeatedly: in the synagogues an
public gatherings often to the point of violence and hatred
His patience was long, and when he turned eventually t
other places and to more teachable people, it was always i
search of maximum opportunity, and never in resentment
or defeat.

Harder still to bear was rejection by fellow Christians, an
especially by his own converts, yet even this came upon him
Dr. Glover gathers into one dreadful list the recorde
criticisms voiced against Paul by his "Christian" opponents
he did not do many miracles, nor have enough visions; h
was not really like an apostle; he was of inexcusably mea
appearance; he sought to please men; he did not write as h
felt; he tricked people with his cunning; he was much to
impulsive, and showed signs of being wrong in the head
From his repeated repudiations, it would seem that som
whispered that he preached for what he got out of it. Whe
Paul defends himself against such antagonism, it is usuall
by the recital of facts, occasionally with a forceful irony
but never with mere retaliation, or mere bitterness. Hi
replies are further evidence of a fine spirit.

Most of these criticisms are gathered from correspondenc
concerned with the tragic breach between Paul and the Cor
inthian Church. Into that painful episode we cannot ente
with full assurance: immaturity, intellectual pride, immoral
ity, disorder, called for plain speaking, and some in th
Church refused his counsel, and rejected his authority. W
can see from his later comments how deeply hurt, t
"anguish, distress, and many tears", Paul had been: his de
sire to visit Corinth conflicting with his resolve not to g
where he was not welcome.

The figure that emerges from this unhappy record is o
one who, charged with grave responsibility, and fully ade
quate to maintain it, yet pleads, beseeches, and persuades, wit
love and pastoral concern — his own pride set aside and hi
own hurt hidden, until the trouble be past. Only a trul

humble spirit can so bear with the follies and sins of lesser, and ungrateful, men.

It would be false to plead that anything of harshness in Paul's character should be excused on the ground that he was often a sick man. One shudders to think what Paul would say to such a plea! Yet his superb handling of personal affliction is surely something to be remembered in estimating his personal qualities.

Doubtless it is well we do not know precisely what Paul's trouble was – his "stake (or, thorn) in the flesh". By his own confession we know it was painful, persistent, disabling, and distressing, producing weakness and infirmity. We know he prayed concerning it, three times, and with passion. And we know the request was refused. Instead, Paul received the promise of grace sufficient for edurance; insight to discern the lesson of the experience – to prevent his becoming unduly elated by his many visions and revelations of the Lord – and the discovery that as the affliction kept him harassed and humbled it led in fact to a yet greater manifestation of the power of Christ.

This paradoxical result was partly due to the effect of his infirmity upon those who considered "his bodily presence weak and his speech of no account", yet who were compelled to acknowledge the forcefulness of his personality. His strength was obviously not his own. But it was also due to the sustained and humble dependence on the daily strength of Christ, which affliction made necessary. The apostle had the wit, and the humility, to recognise what his namesake, the king of Israel, only discovered too late, that to be little in one's own eyes is to enjoy the favour of the Almighty.

A prevailing gentleness of spirit, an unbreakable courage of heart, an underlying humility of soul, provide the basis for that extraordinary public career. Those who take time to read the motives behind the controversies, to feel the heartbeats beneath the armour, to measure the saintliness that so refined this man's indomitable strength, can only wonder at the moral miracle which grace wrought in Paul's mighty soul – wonder, and envy.

11 *His Consecration: "To Me to Live Is Christ"*

IT IS IMPOSSIBLE to explain Paul entirely in terms of th
faith he held, of the spiritual experience he shared, of th
character he possessed, or even of all three together. It i
true that he personifies powerful and far-reaching ideas
that he lived from a profound depth of religious life; that hi
personal qualities were such as to kindle intense admiratio
and endear him to many. Yet there is more to this man tha
belief, piety, and virtue: he is a man at strain, in ever
sense a man possessed, a man devoted, a man in love.

That ruthlessness which has been remarked, about Paul'
logic and about his ethical demands, is stamped also upo
his own intense passion for Christ. Decision, commitmen
consecration, are insufficient words to describe Paul's burnin
loyalty to Jesus: he shows an unsparing singleness of purpose
a consuming wholeheartedness, for which the only adequat
illustrations are the total concentration of the trained athlete
the unquestioning submission of the slave, the entire devotio
of a sacrificial victim, the compulsive absorption of the lover

Yet, while the descriptions and comparisons tend of neces
sity to become emotional, it is imperative to notice tha
in Paul's mind these metaphors, and the attitudes the
express, have essentially practical, material, and even earthy
applications.

Athlete

The intense concentration of the runner is well convey
in Paul's words to the Philippians: "I press on . . . One thin
I do, forgetting what lies behind me and straining forwar
to what lies ahead, I press on toward the goal for th
prize . . ." — and what Paul was seeking to forget, an
what to attain, we can well guess. This is still Paul's spiri
and temper in advancing years. Not very long before, o
the road up to Jerusalem, he had enshrined his attitude t
life, and to the dangers ahead of him, in similar language
declaring that his life held no other value for him tha
that he might finish his appointed course and complet
his race.

One of Paul's last notes echoes the same thought. Within the shadow of death he pens a phrase that seems to recall the relay race of the Greek games in far-back Tarsus: I have finished my lap; I have carried the baton of the faith for the appointed distance; henceforth others run, but for me, a crown.

In all three passages, the implications of this frame of mind are practical enough. He is facing the finishing tape, which for him appears to mean the executioner's sword. He desires above all else grace to stay the distance and run well to the end. Years earlier the same athletic concentration was applied to personal problems of self-discipline. Writing of his strenuous inward conflicts, he recalls that though all runners compete, only one receives the prize, and that athletes accept the severest disciplines of self-control merely in hope of a perishable chaplet of victory: "Well, I do not run aimlessly, I do not box as one beating the air; But I pommel my body and subdue it, lest after preaching to others I myself should be disqualified."

"I run . . . I box . . . I pommel my body . . . I press toward the mark . . . I will finish my course . . ." To modern ears, of course, games-metaphors are perfectly familiar, altogether appropriate, even hackneyed, in religious exhortation. They were firmly barred, by their Gentile associations, from most Hebrew teaching. They are peculiarly Paul's: borrowed, it may be, as to language, from his boyhood environment, but born so far as Christian literature is concerned in the consuming eagerness of Paul's spirit, in his passionate heart's all-out striving after goals far out of reach but nevertheless demanding unlimited and unending endeavour. Faced with temptation or with danger, Paul's consecration to the Christian way allowed neither measure nor caution: his soul ran after Christ, and would not be hindered.

Slave

Spiritual athleticism, however, expresses only a very small part of Paul's attitude towards Christ. It omits entirely the dimension of unquestioning obedience which is so obviously an integral part of his consecration. Here, the far less congenial metaphor of slavery is unavoidable, and too frequently upon Paul's lips to be evaded. He is the "bondslave of

Christ", and from the way in which he contrasts spiritua and literal slavery, and draws out its implications, there ca be no question that he chooses the figure in full view of it more horrible associations.

Paul bears on his body the marks of Jesus, and is "sealed" (as a purchase) with Christ's Spirit. He is answerable, no to human commands or criticism but to his own Master, i heaven. He, like his readers, has been purchased, and i no longer his own; he has been "redeemed" – a slave-marke term in the first century – and Jesus is now his "Lord".

It is instructive to compare Paul's introduction of himsel in his various epistles: as "apostle" when he is to writ things not altogether welcome, or easy to accept; as "bond slave of Christ" when in the closer intimacy of mutual trus he can say what is nearest to his heart. He felt nothin repugnant in so describing Christ's mastery over him. "H gave himself for me" – that constituted a right of absolut possession which Paul unhesitatingly conceded.

In applying this conception to his readers (and doubtles to himself) Paul contended that sexual immorality was kind of stealing. You are not your own, to do as you wil with your lives, or even with your bodies, for you ar Christ's, and not to be shared with harlots! With equal real ism, in a very different sphere of thought, Paul held tha acceptance of the slave's position conferred a measure o protection: on the storm-tossed ship in mid-Mediterranea he could speak with confidence of his ultimate safety be cause of the word of "the God to whom I belong" – a a precious possession not lightly to be lost.

But the strongest implication of this way of defining Paul' devotion to Christ lies in the obvious function of the slave to work, and to do so as the Master alone directs. "Woe i me if I do not preach . . . Necessity is laid upon me . . . I am entrusted with a commission." To be alive at all, h tells the Philippians, means for me fruitful labour.

For Paul, the meaning of consecration was not exhauste by intense spiritual feelings, or pious moods, by larg promises and dreams of Christian achievement that evaporat in moving hymns or dissolve in secret tears. His was a robust conception of surrender, that yielded up to Chris time and energy, and concentration of mind, and strengt of body. He was at Christ's disposal, under Christ's command, about his Lord's business and on his Master's errands, the slave of Jesus to be sent or stayed, used or laid aside in gaol, as the Master pleased. Never in all history did a slave more eagerly declare, "I love, I love my Master, I will not go out free."

Sacrifice

There is yet a quality in Paul's personal consecration which neither ardent endeavour nor complete submission sufficiently describes: it has also a deeply religious tone, to express which the sacred metaphor of sacrifice is essential. For always to Paul's mind Christ is divine: His claim rests upon more than the moral right of love or purchase, it is absolute and unarguable, because it is of God.

In the most explicit way, and again with very practical and concrete issues in view, Paul contrasts the symbolic worship of the ancient Temple, with its substitute-sacrifices and its emblematic offerings, with the actual, living offering of the Christian's body, a "living sacrifice", holy, and acceptable to God, which constitutes truly spiritual worship.

To appreciate the power of such an image over Paul's mind one must remember his native and nurtured reverence for all the rich ceremonial of Jewish worship, his unhesitating acceptance of the divine authority and the profound truth of man's sacrificial approach to God, and his adherence, even to the end, to all that remained valuable for Christian hearts in the Temple discipline. The death of Christ for sin was to Paul's mind illumined and explained by sacrificial language; for God has "put forward" Christ as an expiation by His blood, a sacrifice offered in view of our sin. Christ our Passover has been sacrificed for us.

The idea was therefore, for Paul, no worn and defaced coin of ancient religious tender, but a vivid and appealing key-word calling up a train of powerful and holy associations linked to all that belonged to his earliest fearful and awe-struck attendance upon the Temple ritual. The sweetness of the harvest offerings lingers in his imagination as he describes the gifts of the Philippians, "a fragrant offering, a sacrifice acceptable and pleasing to God." But usually it is the animal bound with cords to the horns of the altar, the entire dedication to God symbolised in the surrender of its life, the outpouring of its blood in solemn libation before Him who first gave life and has unanswerable right to receive it again, that is recalled. As did Christ for us, so must we "present our bodies, a living sacrifice" in spiritual worship of the Most High.

So Paul binds himself to the horns of God's altar: "I am already on the point of being sacrificed; the time of my departure has come." "Even if I am to be poured as a libation upon the sacrifical offering of your faith, I am glad, and rejoice with you all." Christ's claim over him had all the absoluteness of God's command; and it involved also that the sacrifice be *holy* – no maimed or blemished offering, but the perfect, continual worship of a complete and unsullied life. In this light of ancient ritual and holy adoration, Paul saw the service of God as a consecration of the whole self which must be measured, not by what it costs us, or how it compares with what others do, or with what we might have done: it must be measured only by how far it is worthy of Him to whom in loving and reverent devotion it is solemnly dedicated. To live for Christ *is* to worship God.

Lover

If the analysis of Paul's consecration is to be complete to the striving, the obedience and the devotedness must be added the fourth, entirely personal, dimension of love. All the affective elements of Paul's deeply emotional nature were quickened and focussed by Jesus. Paul himself would probably not express the matter that way: he would certainly emphasise that the love he felt towards Christ was only the reflection, automatic but inadequate, of Christ's love for him, the love of God towards himself now poured into his heart by the Holy Spirit.

The love of Christ, received, becomes within the soul a motive force of immense power, and we cannot rightly assess Paul's public ministry without reckoning realistically with this constraint of love which he confesses. But even confining attention here, so far as possible, to his more private discipleship, we may notice that love for Christ operated within Paul's heart in two distinct ways.

On the one hand Paul so loved Christ as to find in Him all the delight, and joy, and gladness, of his soul. Paul *enjoyed* Christ. "Rejoice in the Lord always" is one of his characteristic exhortations, and possessing that undying source of joy, he could cry, "Rejoice evermore!" He rejoiced that Christ was preached, he rejoiced in hope in Christ, he exulted in the joy of faith resting upon Christ.

This delight in Jesus, the felt blessing of love received and love returned, was one of the deepest impulses of his life. Unless we evaluate it fully, we might suppose his intense consecration to have been wholly austere and forced – which it certainly was not. He could well have written

Then why, O blessed Jesus Christ,
Should I not love Thee well?
Not for the sake of winning heaven
Or of escaping hell;
Not with the hope of gaining aught,
Nor seeking a reward,
But as Thyself hast loved me,
O ever-loving Lord.

In this rapture of enjoying faith Paul is exactly described as a man in love.

But that love operated also, as true love always does, as a moral incentive to be worthy of the loved One. Paul needed no reminder that none can be worthy of the free gift of divine grace. But it is possible to prove worthy of the trust already reposed in one, of the free gift already undeservedly received. So Paul prays often that his converts shall be worthy of their calling, worthy of the gospel, shall not eat or drink at the Lord's Table unworthily of what they there commemorated.

Most surprisingly, Paul urges the Colossians to lead a life worthy of the Lord, and the Thessalonians to lead lives worthy of God. In slightly different phrase, to "please" God is the assumed desire of the spiritual man; to "please the Lord" is a consideration urged in connection with the decision whether or not to marry; and to please, and to be worthy of, are deliberately linked in the phrase "worthy of the Lord unto all pleasing".

Of his own controlling ambition the apostle can ask, with

a tone of indignant repudiation, "Am I now seeking the favour of men, or of God? Or am I trying to please men? If I were still pleasing men I should not be a servant of Christ." Again, to the Thessalonians, "As we have been approved by God to be entrusted with the gospel, so we speak, not to please men, but to please God who tests our hearts."

To aim to be worthy of the Christ we follow, and thereby to bring pleasure to Him "Whom thy soul loveth", is the natural language of the heart, however odd it may sound theologically. And Paul, whose deepest delight was in Christ, aimed by every opportunity life afforded of living worthily and to Christ's pleasure, to return something of that delight to Him who loved beyond all telling – and beyond all return.

When all metaphors are dropped, and Paul's inner consecration is stated in uncoloured language as simple fact, only one expression will do: to me to live is Christ. Everything else is here: the striving to attain to Christ, as the goal of all spiritual ambition; the entire obedience to Him as the one Master whose word is truth and whose will is law; the limitless dedication of life as a sacrifice reverently laid upon the altar of His cause; the love that so identifies itself with Him that life without Him seems empty and wholly meaningless.

To me to live is Christ – to live from Christ, as the Source, the Author, of life; to live for Christ, as the One alone worth serving; to live by Christ, strengthened with His might and endued with the power of His resurrection; to live unto Christ, as ideal, and standard, and example, and end. Such was Paul's life. If he worked at a trade, it was to bring his fellow-craftsmen to Christ, the Carpenter. If he travelled Asia Minor, Macedonia, Greece, and dreamed of the far West, it was only that he might add fresh realms to Christ's kingdom. Driven before the storm in an over-laden vessel, he strives to win the sailors for the Christ who walked the sea and stilled the storm. When he made at last for Rome, he would tell the eternal city of a greater King than Caesar.

All centres in Christ, for Paul; and in Christ not as a fleeting memory, a portrait loved and studied, the personification of his own conscience, the objectifying myth embodying a mystical faith – it is foolish and stultifying to foist such abstractions upon Paul! For him, Jesus is first a historical figure, crown and culmination of a long historical process, and now still (so to speak) historical in an eternal dimension, a "living, bright, reality,"

Centre and soul of every sphere –
Yet, to each loving heart, how near!

For Paul, life began in the apprehension of Christ, aims at the imitation of Christ, is directed by identification with Christ, is sustained by union with Christ, rejoices in the expectation of Christ. F. W. H. Myers in no way exaggerates Paul's meaning, that to live *is* Christ:

Yea, thro' life, death, thro' sorrow and thro' sinning
He shall suffice me, for He hath sufficed:
Christ is the end, for Christ was the beginning,
Christ the beginning, for the end is Christ.

That is consecration.

12 His Companions: "My Fellow Workers"

THE QUALITY of a man's companions is an index, and their number is in some sense a measure, of his soul. The deepest friendships must always be few, and in the case of gifted and powerful personalities, probably fewer still. Yet a man's power to attract and harness others to his own ideals, his positive contribution to others' lives, his appreciation of other types of people, are reliable indications not only of the breadth of his sympathies but of the genuineness of his self-assessment and the sincerity of his work. And they are indications of character, all the more significant because they are objective, and impossible to counterfeit. One cannot pretend to be a leader of men.

It has often been remarked that Paul was uniquely fortunate in his lieutenants – though to ascribe such a wealth of personal loyalties to "fortune" is scarcely adequate. To notice only the more prominent is to recognize at once their great variety, their high spiritual quality, and their strong devotion to the apostle.

Curiously little known, yet altogether invaluable both to Paul and to the Church, was Silas, a prophet (or preacher) in his own right, an evangelist and fellow missionary of some force, and a sharer with Paul in much tribulation at Philippi, at Thessalonica, at Beroea, and apparently at Corinth – where he disappears from the record of Paul's life. That he was a man of marked personality and recognized position in the Church is sufficiently shown by his being sent, by the Jerusalem Church Council, as one of the two emissaries to Antioch, bearing the Council's decision on the admission of the Gentiles and charged to explain and defend it to the brethren there.

The intention behind this commission was to make clear that the favourable report of the Council by Barnabas and Paul carried the full authority of the Jerusalem Church, and this seems to imply that Silas would be recognised as one of the original Jerusalem circle. If "apostles of Christ" is to be understood in its usual sense, Silas must also have seen the risen Lord. The alternative form of his name, Silvanus, serves to remind us that he, like Paul, was a Roman citizen. He is thus on every count an appropriate colleague for Paul to choose to replace Barnabas, and later to be left behind to oversee and consolidate the work in Macedonia.

It has been suggested that the prophetic inspiration of Silas was the means by which Paul was guided away from Asia and Bithynia and drawn to Troas and Philippi – which would greatly increase the Church's already heavy debt to him. Silas and Timothy are associated with Paul as joint authors of the letters to the Churches they had founded, and the contribution of Silas to the contents of the letters is thought to have been much more than that of mere scribe, or secretary. It is very probable that to his skill in the Greek language Peter's epistle also owes a great deal.

We may surely assume that the warmheartedness and earnest moral counsel of the epistles he helped to write reveal the man. Long and close collaboration would make Paul confirm Peter's commendation of Silas as "a faithful brother". That he was an older man, and less gifted than his great leader, seems not to have mattered: Paul found in him a loyal and trusted friend, and a full partner in the energetic years.

Timothy was younger, a convert of Paul's at Lystra, and "well spoken of by the brethren both at Lystra and Iconium", which suggests some service given to both Churches. Almost every notice of Timothy implies some weakness or timidity, the need to assert his authority, to disregard his youthfulness, and to care for his health. Paul speaks of him as "my beloved and faithful child in the Lord . . . my own son", and with unusual feeling commends him to the Philippians in moving words: "I have no one like him, who will be genuinely anxious for your welfare . . . But Timothy's worth you know, how as a son with a father he has served with me in the gospel."

In similar manner Paul prepares Timothy's way in the Church at Corinth: "When Timothy comes, see that you put him at ease among you, for he is doing the work of the Lord as I am. So let no one despise him. Speed him on his way in peace." That exhortation reveals as much about Timothy as it does of the Church at Corinth, and the same impression of a want of personal force is gained from Paul's repeated words of encouragement, and his reminding Timothy of his early training in Hebrew piety (although his parentage was mixed Jewish-Greek), and his first experiences of persecution and Christian stedfastness in his native cities.

Despite this temperamental handicap, Timothy replaces John Mark as junior companion to wait upon Paul's more domestic needs, and he is soon found accepting responsibility with Silas for consolidating work already begun, while Paul forges ahead. Later he is sent to try to settle the incipient trouble at Corinth, and he twice visited that Church with Paul. Among other tasks Paul entrusted to him was to help organise the collection for Judea's poorer Churches, and with Erastus he was sent to further establish the Churches in Macedonia. He appears to have been ministering at Ephesus during the later years of Paul's life, rejoining Paul at Rome during his recorded imprisonment, and himself suffering imprisonment there.

Paul always spoke of Timothy with affection and intimate trust, and commended him to the Churches as well able to interpret his own mind and teaching, and as an example to the brethren of the ideals Paul would have them follow. Of the deep attachment of the young worker to the apostle there is no doubt. It speaks much for Paul's tenderness and patience that he retained so long the loyalty of a timid soul constantly in need of encouragement; and that Timothy, under Paul's forceful leadership, achieved so much for the cause of Christ.

Of the gracious, liberal-minded physician Luke, we are better informed from his own very beautiful writings than from recorded events. He joined Paul on the second missionary tour, remained one of his travelling party for much of the subsequent evangelistic journeyings, and is found still at Paul's side during his imprisonment at Rome.

A Gentile, and possibly (like many physicians) a freed slave, Luke reveals a trained and acute mind, an excellent mastery of Greek, a broad sympathy, and an informed appreciation of the appeal which the better type of Judaism, and its heir and fulfilment in Christianity, could make to cultured and aristocratic Gentiles. Luke shows, indeed, a very considerable skill as advocate for the defence, not of Paul only, but of Christianity itself.

It is surely significant that Paul could hold within his inner circle of friends, Silas, a Jew of the original Jerusalem Church, and Luke, a Gentile imbued with the widest culture and outlook; and harness them alike, and together, to his cause of world-Christianity.

Other figures have their exits and their entrances on the Pauline stage, some far more important to Paul, and to the story of the Church, than the brief and largely accidental references to them might suggest. One such is Tychicus, an Ephesian and a representative of the Church at Ephesus in carrying the collection to Jerusalem. He was companion or messenger of the apostle as occasion required, and supported Paul at Rome, "a beloved brother, and faithful minister in the Lord; a fellow servant."

Concerning Aristarchus, Dr. Glover remarks that "whenever he is mentioned one regrets that we do not know more." A Thessalonian, he became dangerously, and courageously, involved in the riot at Ephesus, and is found beside Paul again during the imprisonment at Caesarea, probably on the journey to Rome, and certainly later when during his imprisonment there Paul wrote to Colosse. A "fellow prisoner", and a very present friend in trouble!

Epaphras of Colosse may well have been Paul's representative in founding the Colossian Church during the apostle's Ephesian campaign. Bringing news of the Church to Paul at Rome, he remains there to care for the aged prisoner. Paul warmly commends him as an earnest pastor, zealous, and fervent in prayer for his far-away flock: and more personally, speaks of him with affectionate pleasure as a "beloved fellow bondsman and fellow captive".

Epaphroditus of Philippi is another "brother, and fellow worker, and fellow soldier", possibly the "true yoke fellow" mentioned in the Philippian letter. He bore the affection and gifts of the Philippian Church to the apostle at Rome, and he, too, stayed on in the capital to express the concern of his Church in practical service for Paul, and also in helping to evangelise the city. His labours exhausting his physical strength, an almost fatal illness ensued, causing Paul much concern and threatening "sorrow upon sorrow". On his recovery, Paul sent him back to Philippi as much for rest as to allay the Church's anxiety. So another disappears from the occasional record, but as has been well said, he leaves "a fragrant memory of self-forgetful and self-sacrificing devotion, at once to the person of Paul and to the cause of Christ."

Titus was a Greek, probably a convert of Paul's, and a leader well known in Galatia. He was a "partner and fellow helper" to whom difficult tasks could be assigned — an illuminating glimpse into his character. He was more successful than Timothy in resolving the problems at Corinth; he was appointed to Crete to set in order the things needing attention in that unpromising field; and he was called urgently to Paul's side in the final crisis. Could it be that even the apostle, ageing and in peril, longed for one among his companions stronger than Timothy or Luke, upon whom he could lean and in whose tenacity he could renew his own?

What would we not give to learn more of Paul's two fellow craftsmen, Aquila and Priscilla his wife? The details are so scanty, the allusions so provoking of curiosity, and what is not told was yet so obviously important in the development of those early Churches. Aquila was a Jew of Pontus, and with his wife is often thought to have belonged to distinguished social circles in Rome before being banished from the capital with all other Jews under the edict of Claudius. They came to Corinth, where Paul met them and stayed with them. Since the expulsion from Rome arose from synagogue disturbances about one "Chrestus", it seems likely that the couple were already Christians — as Paul's choosing to lodge with them might seem to confirm.

Returning to Ephesus with Paul, they were persuaded to remain there to initiate Christian work in that great city, and have share in leading Apollos into a more perfect understanding of the gospel. Paul's commendation of this able, experienced and valuable pair is unusually free and heartfelt: "My fellow workers in Christ Jesus, who for my life laid down their own necks, unto whom not only I give thanks, but also all the Churches of the Gentiles." Here plainly is one of Christianity's unwritten stories. But whether Paul is thinking of some special heroism, or of the total contribution of this devoted couple to his widely scattered mission field, the bond between these and the apostle is yet another example of the power of Paul to attract and hold great personal loyalty while remaining acutely appreciative of all that others did for him.

Around the better known figures, however, is a far larger circle of colleagues scarcely recognisable; well over sixty have been counted who shared in varying degrees the life and work of Paul. Long lists of greetings that open or close his epistles enshrine their names and his grateful affection. This great capacity for friendship is part of the explanation of this feature of Paul's life. He held the love of young men: Onesimus, the runaway slave, who would have stayed beside the old prisoner in Rome if Paul had consented, and Timothy, and Mark, and Epaphroditus, are examples. As G. B. Caird well says, "Men always love and admire those who bring out the best in them." But Paul held older men, too, as Philemon, Silas, and probably Tychicus.

The chapter that closes the epistle to the Romans contains abundant evidence that Paul's was a "much more deeply affectionate and sympathetic nature than we sometimes think" — and that he was a shrewd assessor of others' quality and work. Phebe the deaconness has been "a helper of many, and of myself as well"; Epaenetus is remembered as the first Asian convert; Mary "has worked hard among you"; Andronicus and Junias are Paul's kinsmen and fellow prisoners, older in Christ than Paul, and men of note among the apostles.

Ampliatus is "beloved", as also is Stachys, and Urbanus is a fellow worker in Christ. Appelles is "approved in Christ" — what story lies embalmed in that phrase? The families of Aristobulus and of Narcissus are remembered; so is Herodion, and so again is the work of the women Tryphaena and Tryphosa. The "beloved Persis" has "worked hard in the Lord"; Rufus is "eminent in the Lord", and "his mother — and mine" is sent especial greeting.

Nine others are simply named, but in two house-groups, or "cells". Three of Paul's kinsmen are mentioned, with Gaius "who is host to me and to the whole Church", Erastus the city treasurer, and "our brother" Quartus.

The same particularity, and gratitude, mark all the greetings lists, and show a heart that treasured each human contact, and held undimmed the memory of the person, the circumstances, and the character of each fellow Christian.

It was this faculty for friendship, and not simply good fortune, that made Paul blessed in his comrades.

And the same natural gift for friendship kept him from losing the colleagues he made. Once he speaks somewhat acidly of those who "all look after their own interests, not those of Jesus Christ", and this seems to refer to those in Rome who "proclaim Christ out of partisanship, not sincerely but thinking to afflict me in my imprisonment", possibly the "dogs . . . evilworkers" the "concision-party" of Judaist Christianity. But this tone is exceptional. Demas, too, "in love with this present world" has forsaken Paul's team, and the apostle's regret mingles with his rebuke. The general impression is of great and lasting personal loyalty, and to this Paul himself unquestionably contributed by his high valuation of his friends.

He repeatedly associates with himself in the authorship of his various letters the colleagues present with him at the time, adding their greetings conjointly, and as on equality with his own. He shows no apostolic "side" — if there could be such a thing. He shows no jealousy, either: the Corinthians' favourite, Apollos, is like himself a servant of God, his "watering" as necessary as Paul's "planting" if God is to give the increase. He could so easily have contributed to a fierce quarrel at Corinth by unguarded words of praise for his own adherents, but he contemptuously repudiates all cliques, and all personal adulation. All ministers of the gospel, Paul, Apollos, Cephas, and the rest, all are "yours" to benefit from, and to thank God for.

When it is necessary, Paul asserts his independence of Peter, James, and John, yet he betrays no envy or disparagement — except to criticise Peter's obvious inconsistency of conduct at Antioch. His tribute to Mark helped much to erase the effects of Mark's early mistake; his warning to put Timothy at his ease at Corinth likewise reveals the strength and care of his own loyalty to younger colleagues. Such actions made others feel they could trust his friendship, even as he knew he could rest in theirs, and his own loyalty cemented spiritual fellowship into a bond which no criticism or adversity could break.

Yet a third factor in this gregarious dimension of the apostle's character must be named, although it has often been emphasised since Dr. Glover drew attention to it. It is Paul's great fondness for words which include a prefix signifying "togetherness" – frequently words of his own somewhat clumsy coining. The list of such expressions in his writings is astonishing. If we attempt to convey Paul's forceful meaning by the strong, archaic English word "fellow", with its associations of "one of a pair", "comrade", "counterpart", "partners in investment", and the like, then Paul speaks of Christians as

fellow athletes
fellows in burial (of baptism)
fellow components (of building)
fellow corporate (blended together in one body)
fellows in death
fellow groaning
fellows in the heavenlies
fellow heirs
fellows in life
fellow partakers
fellow refreshed
fellow rejoicing
fellow servants
fellow soldiers
fellow sympathisers
fellow workers
and even "fellows in fellowship"

fellow built
fellow citizens
fellow comforters
fellow contenders
fellow crucified
fellows in glory
fellow growing
fellow helpers
fellow imitators
fellow minded
fellow prisoners
fellow reigning
fellow risen
fellow sharers
fellow sufferers
fellow travailers
fellow yoke-bearers

As a point of linguistic style, indicating a prevailing tendency of Paul's thought, this list is interesting: but it betrays more a theological than a merely literary trait. This is part of Paul's whole interpretation of Christianity. As has been said, he saw the Church as essential to the purpose of Christ; he interpreted conversion as a call to fellowship; he believed love – necessarily a communal virtue – to be the law of Christ; and he held that only together could Christians learn, grow, and live in the will of Christ.

Paul's capacity for friendship sprang thus not only from natural gifts of personality, or from self-discipline in personal relationships, or even from wide and deep experience of the value of spiritual fellowship, but from conviction about the nature of the gospel. His message of Christ was a principle of reconciliation among men, as well as between men and God; the saving experience of Christ was far too rich and many-sided to be explored in isolation; and the grace and glory of Christ no one mind or heart or life could encompass or comprehend alone.

And up the radiant peopled way
That opens into worlds unknown
It will be life's delight to say,
"Heaven is not heaven for me alone".

Rich by my brethren's poverty? —
Such wealth were worthless! I am blest
Only in what they share with me,
In what I share with all the rest.

13 *His Citizenship: "I Appeal to Caesar"*

THE PERPETUAL TEMPTATION of all ardent religion is to forget this world. An evangelical zeal like Paul's, concentrated upon spiritual aims, consecrated to the service of a risen Lord, is only very rarely combined with worldly realism and practical common sense – and the combination, when it does occur, is formidable! Paul's head was often in theological clouds, and his heart always in heaven with Christ: but his feet were firmly on the ground, his faith and ideals harnessed to purposes that had to do with a Church still on earth, and with saints struggling with the assaults of a virulently pagan society, with Caesar's military dictatorship, and a whole world urgently needing to be redeemed.

Symptomatic of this realistic awareness of facts, even of unwelcome facts, is Paul's readiness to take advantage of the existing elements in his situation even when they were the result of circumstances or policies he would denounce. Thus Rome was a pagan Empire, often ruthlessly oppressive and sometimes cruel: but that was no reason for ignoring the exceptional opportunities offered to Christian evangelists by the strategic system of communications that spanned Rome's world. The opposing factions of Pharisee and Sadducee in the supreme Council of his nation must often have frustrated progress, and weakened seriously Judaism's policy in dealing with her overlords: yet Paul cleverly uses his inside knowledge of the situation within the Sanhedrin to divide his enemies amongst themselves.

So, too, in spite of the strong opposition he raised to making Jewish customs obligatory for Gentile Christians, he is at once aware of the expediency of circumcising Timothy to ensure admission to Jewish circles; and of the advantages in Jerusalem of conforming to the ritual laws and of performing a popular act of charity by paying the vow-fees of poorer Jews. Similarly, he knows how easily he might sway the emotions of a patriotic Jerusalem mob into his own favour, if he addresses them, while obviously a prisoner taken by the hated Roman force within the Temple precincts, and speaks in their mother-tongue.

The apology of the magistrates at Philippi for their

hasty action against Paul and Silas will help to protect the infant Christian cause Paul leaves there from further annoyance by officials or by popular clamour – so Paul insists that it be made openly, and before witnesses. Stormbound, he calmly and sensibly urges food upon hungry and despondent crew and passengers; his arrangements for the due ordering and government of his new-founded Churches show the same intense practicality of mind in spiritual affairs.

In more purely intellectual matters he is just as realistic. How very differently he approaches a Jewish audience at Pisidian Antioch, a provincial Gentile one at Lystra, a University campus at Athens! In all his speeches and letters he manifests an astonishing range and skill, and a wise shrewdness in appealing to the characteristic predilections and resistances of different types of people. Always he understands thoroughly his human targets – Agrippa, Festus, the Corinthian Church, the Philippians, the peoples of Galatia, the Romans. When he so wishes, he can be exceedingly tactful, as in his approach to Churches he had not founded.

When discussing detailed problems of applying Christianity to everyday life in a great heathen city, Paul reveals a clear grasp both of the concrete difficulties and of the essential principles involved. In nothing does this man suggest to our minds the absent-minded theologian, or the withdrawn and other-worldly hermit. He is alert, awake, and very much on terms with the world in which he lives and to which he ministers. Paul is no man's fool – least of all the world's.

Negative

There is, nevertheless, in Paul's teaching about Christian social relationships a note of warning and withdrawal. To deny this is as one-sided as to exaggerate it, as though "separation" were all Paul had to say. It was entirely necessary to warn young converts in a heathen environment to make a clean break with evil, to tolerate no compromise with ways of sin: "What partnership have righteousness and iniquity? What fellowship has light with darkness? What accord has Christ with Belial? Or what has a believer in common with an unbeliever? . . . Therefore come out from them, and be separate from them, says the Lord, and touch nothing unclean . . ."

The Thessalonian Church is warned against the slumbering and drunkenness characteristic of "sons of darkness and of night", and urged to do not "as others do"; the Ephesians are reminded that they once shared the passions and disobedience of "the rest of mankind", and now must "take no part in the unfruitful works of darkness, but instead expose them." The Roman Church is similarly warned that the approaching Day of Christ must sharpen the distinction between the Christian and the unbeliever, and "revelling and drunkenness . . . debauchery and licentiousness, quarreling and jealousy" must be put away. Paul can even commit himself to the sweeping judgment, "This present evil age . . ."

The deepest reasons for this attitude, in Paul's writings, are, first, that the world is under judgement. The wrath of God is revealed against all ungodliness and wickedness of men who suppress the truth. The forbidding picture of social life in the early chapters of Romans illustrates the fact that God has "given men up" to the ways of life that they have chosen: it follows that the Christian must keep himself apart, lest he incur the same judgement.

Secondly, Paul is so completely identified with Jesus, in heart and purpose, that in his eyes a world which has crucified Christ has thereby, in the same moment, crucified itself so far as Paul is concerned: "the world is crucified to me, and I unto the world". Thirdly, Paul insists that the Christian's true citizenship is in the commonwealth of heaven, and that Christian hope looks for a Saviour who will deliver "out of this world". To "mind earthly things" is therefore to cling to that from which Christ seeks to redeem you.

For all these reasons Paul requires of Christians a standard of life far above that accepted by "the world"; he requires indeed "blamelessness". Converts must live "above reproach", "giving no offence to Jews or to Greeks or to the Church of God", and "blameless for the Day of Christ." In the letter to the Philippians the demand is still more sharply phrased: "be blameless and innocent, children of God without blemish in the midst of a crooked and perverse generation."

The world will still criticise, oppose, even persecute: but

the Church must not provide occasion, nor by careless behaviour justify the world's abuse. Rather must the world's judgement of the Christian be kept constantly in mind. While Paul refused to conform to the criticisms voiced by the Corinthian Church, counted it a small thing that men should judge him, and despised being slave to public opinion, yet he knew that the Church's influence depended on general approval of her moral character. Christians must, therefore, "look carefully how you walk . . . not as unwise men but as wise . . . conducting yourselves wisely toward outsiders."

This respect for outsiders' judgement underlies the counsel to take thought for what is noble in the sight of all and by common standards. Unexpectedly, Paul applies this principle to worship, demanding (of the Corinthians) what outsiders and unbelievers will think of the way their services are conducted. "Will they not say that you are mad?" Even here, in a sphere which might have been thought private and domestic to the members only, the world's impressions about Christians must be reckoned with; while in the one matter where calumny most easily prospers, the handling of money, Paul is even more scrupulously careful to arrange that representatives of each Church contributing to the relief of the Judean brethren shall accompany him to Jerusalem to convey the gifts and report back to the donors its safe and honourable distribution. "We intend that no one should blame us about this liberal gift which we are administering, for we aim at what is honourable not only in the Lord's sight but also in the sight of men."

In the same spirit, Christians are repeatedly charged to "do good to all men", and to "live peaceably with all". Even good may be evil spoken of, through misunderstanding, or through failure to count upon the misinterpretation of malicious minds, or sometimes through proud independence that relies on being clear in its own conscience whatever men may think. That may very occasionally be necessary: but Paul felt so great a responsibility for the Christian witness toward the world that he strove to retain the good opinion of just men so long as he could. The Christian answer to opposition was not defiance, or contempt, but a standard of life that silenced false accusation, and a temper of goodwill that disarmed hostility.

Positive

Already therefore we can perceive beneath the more negative warnings about corruption and separation a more positive valuation of society and the life of the world. Christians must live in the world, and the Church is involved therein, for good and ill; within the pagan social context Christian principles are to be worked out and Christian character developed and Christian love expressed. Nothing even remotely resembling the later total withdrawal of the monastries is ever suggested. Rather, the Christian must make his own positive approach to the society around him – "among whom you shine as lights in the world" both "holding fast" (for your own sake) and "holding forth" (for the world's sake) "the word of life." Here the Christian is both example and spokesman to the surrounding darkness, and it is for especial faithfulness in this dual task that the Thessalonian Church is particularly commended.

Evangelists have high place in the list of ministers given by the ascending Christ to the Church, and Timothy is warned to give attention to this outreaching enterprise. Throughout Paul's correspondence with the Churches, it is assumed that a prime incentive of Church life is "to make all men see", for God "desires all men to be saved and to come to the knowledge of the truth." For this purpose the grace of God has appeared for the salvation of all men, and the apostle himself becomes "all things to all men that I might by all means save some." Paul's whole career is the only adequate comment on these words. The world offers, therefore, not only peril and responsibility, but opportunity, and the Christian must grasp it.

Accordingly, as we watch Paul's own relationship to outsiders, and especially to civil and imperial authorities, we find a very positive valuation of society and of Christian citizenship informing his attitudes. Everywhere, at Philippi, Corinth, Ephesus, Jerusalem, Caesarea, on board ship, and at Rome, he submits to the forms of Roman justice when accusations are made against him, having evidently great confidence in the processes of Roman law and in the courts' protection of all who are innocent of civil offence.

His assertion of the privileges of Roman citizenship, when he can thus throw around himself or others the shield of

Roman justice, is significant of his whole attitude. "There is no authority except from God, and those that exist have been instituted by God." (This of Rome!) "Therefore he who resists the authorities resists what God has appointed, and... will incur judgement. For rulers are not a terror to good conduct, but to bad. Would you have no fear of him who is in authority? Then do what is good, and you will receive his approval, for he is God's servant for your good. But if you do wrong, be afraid, for he does not bear the sword in vain; he is the servant of God to execute his wrath on the wrongdoer. Therefore one must be subject, not only to avoid God's wrath, but also for the sake of conscience. For the same reason you also pay taxes, for the authorities are ministers of God, attending to this very thing. Pay all of them their dues, taxes to whom taxes are due, revenue to whom revenue is due, respect to whom respect is due, honour to whom honour is due."

And to the debt of subjection, of taxes, and of respect, it was later believed Paul added the obligation to pray "for kings and all who are in high positions, that we may lead a quiet and peaceable life, godly and respectable in every way. This is good, and it is acceptable in the sight of God our Saviour . . ."

It would be difficult to imagine stronger counsel than this on the values of good citizenship; and it is intriguing to speculate how far Paul would have varied his advice a few years later, when the fairness and impartiality he expected from the Roman rulers gave place to a policy of persecution and suppression. Of his fundamental belief there is no doubt: good government and social order are the will of God, and so demand the Christian's active and ungrudging support. "Remind them to be submissive to rulers and authorities, to be obedient, to be ready for any honest work . . ." Christians have a stake in stable society, that the work of God be unhindered: they have also an obligation to defend all that has divine approval in man's common life.

So Paul is wholly on the side of the forces that make for human welfare. He read Christian duty in social, civic, and humanitarian terms as well as those of piety, faith, and evangelism. With the Old Testament prophets behind him, he could hardly do otherwise: but his attitude is still frequently misread by those who see in his warnings only a pietistic antagonism – or indifference – to the busy world's teeming life.

Definitive

For all this, however, Paul was not misled about the sharp differences between this world and the kingdom of his Christ. He knew that the world considered the gospel "foolishness". He confidently expected that every rule, every authority and power, must at last give way before the rule of Christ, that God may be everything to every one. For the sake of expediency, of conscience, of influence, and of witness, Christians must be *good* citizens in the present world situation. But the present world situation is not final, and sooner or later the issues between Christ and Caesar must be outfaced, and the claim of Christ to universal Lordship established for ever.

There is little question that Paul expected this denouement in the form of a Second Coming of Jesus within his own lifetime, in such manifested glory and power that all issues would be settled and this age, and all belonging to it, pass away. We await a Saviour: "we wait for God's Son from heaven . . . Then comes the end, when he delivers the kingdom to God the Father . . ."

But this expectation lingered, and towards the close of his own career, Paul conceived the issues between Christ and Rome to narrow down, *meanwhile,* to a contemporary question between Church and State – the right of the Church to propagate the gospel in the Roman Empire without hindrance or persecution by Jew or Greek or Roman. The *final* outcome remains in Christ's hands at His coming: the immediate question was Christian support of all that was good in Roman society and government in exchange (so to speak) for the immunity of her spokesmen from interference, and the impartiality of Roman courts in all cases of accusation and oppression.

During his own life-work, this issue had been tested repeatedly before the local courts, at the cost of much physical suffering and peril for Paul, but always with success. The apostle remained free to preach, the Church to live and grow. But at Jerusalem, before riotous Jewish crowds and under the weaker hands of time-serving and even corrupt provincial officials like Festus and Felix, the matter might easily be mishandled to the Church's severe disadvantage. If every individual Christian is to be safe, and every local Christian community is to remain undisturbed, the imperial policy towards the new faith must be defined once and for all, and announced with universal authority, from the highest tribunal in the Empire. So Paul, exercising again the privilege of his Roman freedom, and with supreme strategy of statesmanship, in the widest interests of the Church, cries out in the Palestine court: "I appeal to Caesar!" and the provincial authorities have no alternative in Roman law but to reply, "To Caesar you shall go!"

Details of the outcome are unfortunately obscure. By the time Paul appeared before the Emperor, the imperial policy towards Christianity had hardened, and Paul sealed his life's devotion by "honouring Christ by death". It remains true, however, that the appeal of Paul to Caesar's judgement seat was the highest possible expression of a sense of Christian responsibility to the State and to the Church together. If his confidence in Roman justice was to be disappointed, and if always he had seen behind the earthly power that the world was God's and that its throne belonged from the beginning, as at the end, to his Redeemer-Lord, yet meanwhile he would co-operate to the limit of his power with all just authority, and serve the State with a good conscience for Christ's sake.

Paul never forgot his citizenship in Israel; he never undervalued or repudiated his citizenship of Rome; but he held at all times as first priority his membership of the city of God, and found at last, after a glorious career of which the world was not worthy, that the Christian's dearest citizenship is indeed in heaven.

Paul, Servant of the Kingdom

Who Is Sufficient?

This Ministry

So We Preach

His Letters Are Weighty

For the Defence of the Gospel

14 *Who Is Sufficient?*

A SERIOUS DIFFICULTY besets any attempt to study Paul's service of God's kingdom: the assumption that Paul's time is entirely remote, and wholly different from our own. We tend to idealise the apostolic age, and to suppose that every circumstance connected with Christian work has so changed that the precedents, example, and counsel of the New Testament have lost much of their force for Christ's modern servants.

This is a dangerous assumption in any sphere of Christian thought. It is entirely false in the case of Paul, precisely because he is so strangely modern, and his situation so closely similar to our own. This may be illustrated by isolating certain unchanging parallels between Paul's circumstances and ours, and by indicating certain unvarying paradoxes that in every age are inherent in Christian service.

Perennial Problems

Consumed by a characteristically Jewish passion for righteousness, Paul was sharply conscious at all times of the hostile tone of contemporary society. Paul's picture of his own age is critical, pessimistic, full of foreboding insights. He knew that he lived on a down-curve, beside an ebb-tide in culture, civilisation, and faith. He saw retribution upon sin already at work in the moral rottenness of pagan society, which (in his letter to Rome) he paints in the darkest colours – sensuality, greed, violence, homosexuality, corrupting private life, and inter-class and inter-generation strife disintegrating society, with baseness of mind, impropriety of conduct, "all manner of wickedness, evil, covetousness, malice".

It is a dreadful indictment of an age. Envy, murder, strife, deceit, malignity, gossip, slander, hatred of God, insolence, pride and boastfulness mark men who are "inventors of evil, disobedient to parents, foolish, faithless, heartless, ruthless." Even Jews, claiming to be moral leaders of the world, are included in Paul's sweeping denunciation.

The evangelical mind is prone to pessimistic assessments of the spiritual state of the world, but Gentile satirists and

Jewish observers like ben Zakkai and the author of 2 Esdras were not Christian puritans exaggerating evil, but responsible men sharing to the full Paul's anxiety about the trends of the time. Good citizens had reason to fear the forces of disruption working beneath the surface of Roman order, the "secret force of lawlessness that only Caesar held in check" of which Paul hinted to the Thessalonians. Rome's continued nervousness about Jewish and Christian messianism in Palestine and in the capital shows that she was aware of peril.

Such was the uncongenial atmosphere in which Paul worked. He had Church members pitiably ignorant of the elementary standards of good behaviour – even at meals. "Immoral, idolaters, adulterers, homosexuals, thieves, greedy, drunkards, revilers, robbers – such were some of you"! We sometimes are tempted to complain that we are called to serve Christ in an age of widespread spiritual recession; we recognise truth in the terrible image of these days depicted by an acute modern writer: "We now know that history is . . . a crowd of sleep-walkers striving to climb the down-escalator"; we hear the voice of our time in the words of Bertrand Russell, that only on the firm foundation of unyielding despair can the soul's habitation henceforth be safely built. But this is only Paul's age back again. Other generations may conceivably have had things easier: Paul certainly did not.

Always articulate, often eloquent, and with an irresistible urge to preach, Paul was acutely aware of the serious barriers which hinder communication between believer and non-believer in every age. However baffled we may have felt after trying to make intelligible evangelistic contact with certain modern minds, we have probably never been actually mistaken for gods, as Paul and Barnabas were at Lystra; or for political agitators against established authority, as Paul and Silas were at Thessalonica; or for inventors of new deities – called, curiously, the one Jesus, and the other Resurrection – as the apostles were at Athens. What appalling gulfs of misunderstanding are half-revealed in such episodes! On the most ordinary levels of evangelistic approach Paul seems sometimes to have faced difficulties as impenetrable as ours.

But on the theological level, there was a much more difficult barrier to surmount, in the kind of mental readjustments demanded in presenting a Hebrew faith to a Gentile audience. To compare Paul's sermon at Antioch in Pisidia with his words at Lystra a few Sabbaths later, is to see the process of theological translation at work, as he strives to preach the same message in different terms, upon entirely different foundations, and buttressed by entirely different arguments.

Over the whole field of Christian teaching, a discipline of de-Judaising was essential if Gentiles were to comprehend the faith. Christ, or Messiah, is translated into Lord; Passover ideas melt into Love Feast and Lord's Supper; notions like Priesthood, sacrifice, atonement, become latinised (so to speak) into justification, reconciliation, and the theme of *Christus Victor;* the kingdom of God gives place in part to the religious society or Church; and so with many other ideas and emphases first defined in Jewish terms and needing to be paraphrased in Graeco-Roman thought-forms to be made universally intelligible. What an effort of intellect and sympathy that cost the former Rabbi!

On the deepest philosophical level, Paul was always troubled at having to proclaim a message unacceptable, and even repellent; at having to address minds nourished upon other assumptions, furnished with other categories of thought. He might protest that he determined not to know anything save Jesus Christ and Him crucified, and argue that the wisdom of this world is foolishness with God: but one feels that he protests too much for comfort. The Jewish charge that his message was repulsive, the Greek taunt of stupidity, and accusations like that of Festus that learning had turned his brain, all stung the apostle deeply. All his writings show that he was an argumentative and rational thinker, impatient of ignorance and muddle-headedness: for such a man, gibes against his intellectual competence are exasperatingly painful.

Yet Paul needed not to be told how strange his message sounded. He was only too aware of having to preach in terms belonging to a universe of discourse alien to that in which his hearers were at home. How *could* one expound love among the brothels of Corinth, preach the spirituality of God amid the sensual religiousness of Ephesus, advocate peacemaking and meekness in a Roman barracks, or exalt the divine humility in proud Jerusalem? How could one proclaim equality before God in a slave society? Could it all sound anything but nonsense?

Paul's phrase about the folly of what we preach reveals a whole hinterland of intellectual frustration. Though he rationalised the situation with arguments like "If our gospel is veiled, it is veiled only to those who are perishing. In their case the god of this world has blinded the minds of the unbelievers . . ." yet that harsh doctrine itself shows how very keenly he felt this problem of making the gospel intelligible to an uncomprehending, because intellectually unconditioned, world.

This, too, parallels our situation. Our message is near-nonsense to minds tutored on evolutionary biology, modern cosmology, scientific determinism, and nuclear physics. We broadcast to minds tuned to other wave-lengths, within an intellectual culture coming to be based upon non-Christian assumptions and expressed in non-Christian terms. Those whose staple spiritual diet on Saturday evenings is the popular screen must achieve a very violent mental change of gear before they can sit comfortably in Church on Sunday morning.

For a gulf of incomprehension still stretches between the Word of God and the wisdom of man. "My thoughts are not your thoughts, neither are my ways your ways", saith the Lord even yet. All our conscientious efforts to avoid spiritual jargon, to speak the language of the people, to retranslate the scriptures, will not avail to bridge that gulf: and least of all our modern tendency to turn to the more vague and ill-defined non-intellectual language of colour and symbol in ritualistic religion. The "folly" of what we have to proclaim remains a stumbling block, as it was to Paul.

In a third important respect Paul's situation closely parallels our own. As a man convinced of the reconciling purpose of the gospel, Paul was as painfully aware as we are of the weakening and contradictory divisiveness of Christianity. He saw the yawning division between Jew and Gentile being reproduced within the Church of Jesus, and the arguments, charges and counter-charges arising therefrom dogged him for many years, and disturbed and confused his infant Churches. The Judaist controversy in the first century was no less intractable, frustrating, and seemingly insoluble, than the Catholic-Protestant controversy in the twentieth, and similarly involved with historical circumstances and national characteristics.

Already in Paul's time the melancholy search for formulae of co-existence had begun! Peter, an apostle to the circumcision, Paul, equally an apostle, of course, but he must avoid Peter's sphere of operations and go only to the Gentiles! To read Galatians attentively is to feel afresh what frustrated disappointment this all laid upon Paul's spirit. His indignation in that letter is the measure of his intellectual and spiritual vexation over the inconsistencies of the Church.

But though the Judaist-Gentile division was the more important theologically, that which rent the Church at Corinth was no less a denial of the essence of the gospel. Social snobbery, aggressiveness, the assertion of superior knowledge or spirituality against one's fellow-Christians, greed and ostentation manifest in childish and ill-mannered ways at the very Table of the Lord – we can all imagine the kind of heart-sinking disappointment Paul felt as the story was unfolded, the regretful, impatient "Oh what's the use?" to which even an apostle must have been tempted.

Nor may we shrug the problem away as a mere aberration from the originally pure gospel and an originally united Church. Theological differences arose from circumstances and principles as apprehended by different but equally earnest hearts; the patterns of worship followed at Jerusalem and at Corinth differed as much as do those followed today by "high Catholic" and by "evangelical" groups, and for as solid reasons. To pretend that all the divisions and differences are superficial or sinful is to oversimplify to the point of distortion.

The gospel proclaims reconciliation, fellowship, and love: but it does so on such radical, and even revolutionary, terms that conflict, disagreement, and division are inevitable as the preparation for unity and peace. Wherever Christianity comes, collision with existing codes, standards, ways of life, with historical factors, national character, ancient and traditional modes of thought, is unavoidable. The result can only be challenge, disagreement, and eventual accommodation. So the gospel challenged Judaism, and Judaist Christianity, through much argument, worked out a viable compromise between the truth and the ideal on the one hand and the historical circumstances on the other. So the Church challenged second-century paganism and through great conflict Catholicism worked out the compromise. So later still, Christian philosophy confronted traditional Greek philosophy, and the abstruse, intellectualist creeds are the result – from which most of the radiance of original faith in Jesus has surely faded! Always something is lost, and always there is disagreement, division, conflict – and persecution.

Nor is this all. Christianity is new life, and so demands freedom – of mind, of conscience, of belief and opinion, of decision and responsibility, of loyalty to one's own Master. Life must find expression in variety; and freedom and responsibility are essential to maturity – however untidy and painful the result may be to doctrinaire minds. We have to learn to live with the inherent divisiveness of the gospel, as the deepest testimony to its forcefulness, its truth, and its living power; and to live with it in harmony of spirit. It is not easy, in days of lip-service to a spurious and shallow organisational unity that would compromise on everything and iron out all living variety into dead uniformity.

Yet Paul, too, had to live with it, and to regret very often the additional, wholly unnecessary, even embittered divisions that complicated and weakened still further the impact of the gospel, and contradicted too often the deep unity into which, through upheaval and conflict, Christ leads all who stedfastly believe.

Inherent Paradoxes

Beside such basic problems essentially common to all generations of Christ's servants, there are certain paradoxical demands inherent in all Christian service which the faithful worker has to face and to resolve. Two such paradoxes have especial importance for understanding Paul – and ourselves:

and one is the obvious need for Christian boldness, authority, even self-assertion, combined with the inescapable rule of Christian humility.

Little is achieved by a timid, deprecating, apologetic witness to Christian truth. Within the Christian ministry, and in every position of spiritual responsibility, teaching requires authority, the proclamation of the gospel requires clearness of conviction and positiveness of declaration; leadership requires firmness; pastoral counselling (and indeed all faithful concern for others' happiness and progress) requires unafraid assertion of what we know to be true and right.

Paul can admonish sometimes with great severity. "What do you wish, shall I come to you with a rod, or with gentleness? I am prepared to court-martial everyone who is insubordinate" (so Moffatt translates 2 Corinthians 10:6). "If I boast a little too much of our authority, which the Lord gave for building you up . . . I shall be justified. I warned those who sinned before, and all the others, and I warn them now, that if I come again I will not spare them . . . I write this while I am away . . . that when I come I may not have to be severe in my use of the authority which the Lord has given me . . ."

So, too, in the Thessalonian letters: "Now such persons we command and exhort in the Lord Jesus . . . If any one refuses to obey what we say . . . note that man, and have nothing to do with him . . ." Lest we suppose that this note of authority belongs only to apostles, we may recall the warning to the Corinthians not to despise Timothy, the exhortation to the Philippians to hold such men as Epaphroditus in high honour, and the counsel in the Pastoral epistles about the work of Church officers. These allusions (like the threefold exhortation in the epistle to the Hebrews: "Remember your leaders . . . Obey your leaders and submit to them . . . Greet your leaders . . .") are symptoms of a realised need for authoritative oversight which shall not be wholly lost in the friendliness, the anxiety to please, of the servant of God.

Ministry without authority is pathetic. Yet most Christian workers know the snare of over-confidence, the subtle and persistent temptation "to lord it" over other souls. That loaded phrase of Peter's vividly warns against taking in other lives the place rightfully belonging only to the Lord

Jesus – the essence of blasphemy as well as of pride! We have to remember that "to minister" means just "to serve", as Christ Himself was among us as One that served.

We can hardly deny that we are fallible, or that others are free, in the last resort, to follow or oppose the leadership offered them. It is exceedingly difficult, nevertheless, to keep in mind that the ideal of all Christian work is set for all time in the washing of others' feet; and that within the sphere of Christian fellowship all authority has to be combined with humility, all self-assertion with Christ-like self-emptying.

Paul and Apollos are indeed servants of the living God. Yet "What then is Apollos? What is Paul? Servants through whom you believed, as the Lord assigned to each . . . Neither he who plants nor he who waters is anything." Again, "What we preach is not ourselves, but Jesus Christ as Lord, with ourselves as your servants for Jesus' sake." In this extraordinary mingling of authority with humility, Paul transcends in his own character one of the subtlest of all problems of Christian leadership.

Maybe he was helped in doing so by his realisation of that deeper contradiction in his spiritual life – that he was called, independently and directly, without human aid, to be an apostle, and owed his authority to no man: and yet he was himself dependent for so much of knowledge, experience, and fellowship upon the Church as a whole. A mind which can absorb sincerely both of those truths will have little difficulty about serving the Church boldly with a humble spirit, or serving humbly with all the authority of the everlasting truth.

The second paradox of Christian service is perhaps only a particular instance of the first, but it is important. It is the conflict that often arises between the individual's gifts and capabilities on the one hand, and the over-riding demands of Christ's fellowship on the other.

The service of Christ's kingdom, especially in preaching, teaching, or holding prominent executive office, offers fearful opportunities for showing off. It is in the things in which we are distinguished from others that our individual call to some particular sphere of service usually lies. We are appointed for our special gifts, our "talent", our experience, our superior training, our flair for organisation or for getting on with people, our preaching power, our excellence in creative, artistic, musical, dramatic skills, or our capacity for profound thought and competent study.

All such capabilities constitute our personal stewardship of ourselves, and bring with them individual responsibility towards Christ's cause. Unfortunately, while such gifts create opportunities to show how eager we are to serve our Lord, they offer also equal opportunities to show how much we think of ourselves, to grow in self-esteem, to impose upon our brethren, and sometimes to disdain – even to denigrate – our supposedly less gifted colleagues.

To resist such temptations is not easy. A man must believe that God has called and equipped him for the work to which his hand is set; must feel this is his special sphere and opportunity. Yet pride of ability is the most hateful of all pride. Paul was very sure of the divine election and commission, the ennabling grace and gifts, that underlay all his service; but he was equally sure of the essential oneness of all members in the Body of Christ. Ear, eye, hand, foot are all necessary to wholeness, though differing in function, use, and honour. None dares to say that the other is less valuable to the life of the whole. The individual gifts of Peter, Apollos, Paul are alike contributed to the work of one field, to the progress of one building, and what matters is that both field and building are God's – and without His increase the gifts matter nothing.

Paul was so entirely a team man that it ever astonishes us to read the assertions of his own apostleship which the attitude of others occasionally drags from him. He set so high a value upon his fellow-workers that he is sharply impatient with any attempt to compare Christ's servants one with another – as some at Corinth attempted to do. With tart irony he disclaims: "Not that we venture to class or compare ourselves with some of those who commend themselves;" adding more seriously, "For it is not the man who commends himself that is accepted, but the man whom the Lord commends."

The truth here is that each man is called to his specific Christian work on the basis of his individual gifts and traits: and is expected immediately to sink that individuality in the fellowship of the Church, and in loyalty to all other servants of his Lord. If he fails (or refuses) to do this, there will rapidly be no true fellowship around him, but at best a circle of admiring fans whose adulation of him will contribute nothing to lasting spiritual work, or to the glory of Christ. At worst, he will become that monstrous contradiction in terms – a "Christian" worker with whom none can co-operate or find fellowship, because there is no room in his self-important soul for anyone but himself.

On the other hand, if he does sink his individuality in the needs and common life of the whole Christian fellowship within which God has set him, he is likely sometimes to feel a measure of limitation, of frustration, "the ache of unused capacities", perhaps, or the sore discipline of being patient with the slow-minded and the faint-hearted. Yet if with Paul he can see this self-limitation and discipline as just the price of true fellowship, as but the sacrifice of his special and isolating selfhood so that he might be enriched in the selfless fellowship of the Body of Christ, he will not only render infinitely greater service to the kingdom of God, but he will come to appreciate with gladness and increasing gratitude the contribution each of his colleagues is making to the glorious cause that dwarfs both him and them.

"Who is sufficient for these things?" It must be admitted that such a recitation of the difficulties and paradoxes involved in Christian service is forbidding; it seems to betray the high idealism of the ardent convert, conscious of how much he owes to Christ and determined that Christ shall have all there is of his strength and time and love. If the difficulties were all, this reaction would be justified. Of course there is much else, of joy and blessing, of excitement and often unexpected success, of renewed strength when the heart becomes despondent, and always the sustaining sense of Christ's approval and commission. Yet even while we acknowledge that the resources balance the problems, it is surely well to realise clearly what Christian service demands.

From his very earliest contact with Christianity – the days of his persecuting – Paul learned that "all who desire to live a godly life in Christ Jesus will be persecuted", that "through many tribulations we must enter the kingdom of God", that he must "suffer many things", and a great deal else near to the heart of a heroic faith that never expects Christian discipleship to be easy. It is better to begin soberly, knowing that the way is hard and the work exacting, than to start with ill-considered zeal and a flourish of trumpets, and give up in disillusion and despair before the war is won, the tower built.

Paul, at any rate, faced as difficult an age, as demanding a task, as can ever face us: and he rejoiced in the opportunity so afforded to prove his unbreakable devotion to his Lord.

15 This Ministry

FEW THINGS CHANGE more with the passage of time than the meanings of words: and few words in Christian use have been inverted and transformed more surprisingly than the familiar title "minister". In Christian circles the name is now the symbol of the highest of all privileges. It possesses at once an aura of rank and a halo of sanctity: it denotes a professional status and implies a claim to respectful attention. Outside Christian circles it may often be mocked, but it is still so far honoured that men expect of the minister a higher-than-average standard of morality and of charity, and blame him with exceptional severity if he fails.

Yet the title is derived from the double comparative form of *minus,* meaning *less,* which suggests that it signified originally something like "more and more less"! And the New Testament's equivalent word shares in this humility. It is used of attendants at a banquet, of servants helping at a village wedding, of the menial domestic preparations that Martha made in order that Jesus might eat. To be a minister is to be a servant: nothing more.

When Paul uses the title, this flavour of lowly servitude still clings about it. A "servant (minister) of God" is one who waits upon God's bidding, to do Him service. A "minister of Christ" is simply one attending upon Christ's lightest wish. "Ministers of the new covenant" are those charged, as agents, to operate or fulfil the covenant God has made with man through Christ.

A "minister of the gospel" is, for Paul, not one mediating the gospel to men, but one commissioned to "attend" upon the gospel so as to serve its interests – to explore, expound, and exemplify the message of God as one entirely devoted to making it understood. In Paul's mind this might well stand in contrast to the Jewish scribe's equally intense devotion to the service of the Law, as its appointed agent, defender, and exponent. And so also with Paul's remaining phrase, "minister of the Church": Paul means that apostles, pastors, teachers, evangelists, are "your servants for Jesus' sake", attending upon the welfare of the saints and answerable for their security and progress.

This original nuance of the word deserves to be recalled, not only because it enshrines much of Paul's attitude to his great responsibilities, but also because it emphasises that "ministry" was not, in the apostolic Church, a function of certain believers only, but the obvious duty and privilege of all. Every Christian is a servant – a minister – of God. When therefore we examine Paul's thoughts about "this ministry", and have in mind more modern conceptions of this great calling, we must remember that most of what is said applied originally, and ought still to apply, to everyone engaged *in any way* in the service of Christ.

Metaphors

There is no doubt that Paul kept ever before his mind this truth, that he was only Christ's lowly attendant. But he did not on that account think meanly of the work committed to his hands. "I magnify my ministry" is the watchword he offers to all Christian workers. Paul would certainly insist that a man only does that when in practice he faithfully fulfils the ministry's demands; but the words serve also as a clue to Paul's innermost thinking about Christian service. It is true that a too exalted conception of the dignity of the ministry can destroy a man's influence and corrupt his own spirit: but it is true also that too low a conception can breed slothfulness, a feeling of frustration, a mood of settled despondency that invites – and deserves – failure.

Paul's appreciation of the inherent *spiritual* privilege of being a minister of Christ is expressed in numerous ways. Arguing the right of God's servants to be maintained by the gifts of others, he likens the ministry to a whole range of occupations: to soldiering, to vinedressing, to shepherding and ploughing, to the service of the Temple, and priesthood, and to many others. In the middle of the list, rather less congruously, he mentions the ox that tramples out the corn. Was he thinking, wryly, of his own perpetual trudging along endless Roman roads?

Among all these metaphors for Christian service, the agricultural figures are the most familiar, and in Paul's writings alone they cover the whole process of cultivation. "The plowman should plow in hope", for spiritual harvests are often long delayed, and the slow preparation of the ground is a lonely, unappreciated, and unrewarding aspect of missionary or pastoral labour. The sower, the evangelist "that planteth" seems, in some circumstances, to have the easier task, and to derive greater inspiration from results: but he, too, has his disappointments, and knows in his own heart the spiritual cost of every convert.

"He that watereth", tending the new Christian plants with diligence, offering the detailed instruction, warning, counsel and encouragement without which the new spiritual life would surely wither, needs infinite patience with individuals, and inexhaustible friendship. When the excitements of the great rally and the public occasion are past, it is so often the personal worker who achieves the real miracle that sets a new soul on the King's highway.

Paul mentions, too, the crop-farmer, or husbandman, and he "who plants a vineyard", thinking in each case of the special skill needed to make others bear fruit for God. This corresponds to "the equipment of the saints" which is part of the work of the ministry; the training and encouragement of new workers who in their turn will plough and plant and water in God's vineyard, and bring forth "more fruit". Finally there is the reaper, and the thresher, who work in due season if the rest do not lose heart – the blessed souls whose privilege it is to enter into other men's labours and see the fruit of others' faithfulness ripen under their hands.

Hackneyed, and over-worked as the image now is, it is worthwhile to reflect that this conception of Christian service goes back to Christ's own description of Himself, as sowing the truth of God in the fields of history, a task never finished because needing to be done afresh in each new generation-season. And a task in which the worker is helpless without the creative forces of seed and soil – the gospel and the human heart – which he cannot change, or control. He can only be faithful.

Almost equally hackneyed is the idea of the minister as builder, and the work as "edifying" the body of Christ – a sadly mixed metaphor! The conception of a growing Temple of God, indwelt by the Spirit, replacing the Jerusalem Temple as a habitation of the eternal God in time and history, constructed by the fit framing together of the living stones of Christian souls, and erected upon the one enduring and unchangeable foundation of Jesus Christ, was not originally Paul's idea. It is everywhere in the New Testament, echoed by Matthew, John, and Peter, but most probably derived from Jesus Himself: "On this rock I will build my Church."

Paul's special contribution to the metaphor is twofold. He warns against trying to build the eternal Temple on wrong foundations – upon human wisdom instead of divine truth, or upon works instead of faith, or upon ideas instead of upon living relationship to Christ, or upon the popularity of Christ's servants (Peter, or Apollos) instead of upon the Master alone. "For no other foundation can any one lay than that which is laid, which is Jesus Christ." This had been Paul's unique contribution to the Church at Corinth: "like a skilled master builder I laid the foundation", ensuring thereby that the basis and proportions of the building were right. Thereafter less skilled builders can carry on! But the foundation, nevertheless, is not Paul, nor the work that Paul had done, but Christ.

Paul's other contribution to the Temple-building metaphor for Christian service is the reminder that the Day of Christ will disclose "what sort of work each one has done". The Corinthians were busily comparing the methods and the gifts of Peter, Apollos, Paul; and Paul himself acknowledges that it is possible to erect upon the foundation an edifice of varying styles and materials – gold, silver, precious stones, wood, or even the straw and stubble that with lime-plaster or clay builds quickest of all. But neither speed, nor cheapness, nor appearance, is what really matters in building, but permanence. And the service of the Christian will be tested.

Some kind of spiritual building can be done, using instead of sound theological teaching, plain and faithful moral counsel, simple and dignified worship, the mere wood of high-pressure publicity and self-promotion, the dry hay of clever anecdote and epigram, the stubble of swingtime choruses, sensational public confessions, and nondescript religious clubbery. But "if any man's work is burned up, he will suffer loss . . . If the work which any man has built on the foundation survives, he will receive a reward." The great difficulty is, that it is not easy to work always with only *future* praise in view.

The conception of the minister as soldier is less familiar and much less attractive. But not only does Paul exhort the young pastor Timothy to endure his share of suffering as a good soldier of Christ Jesus, and to leave part-time occupations alone, as a good soldier should: he also reviews his own ministry in military terms. "I have fought the good fight". If the following phrase, "I have kept the faith", is related to this idea rather than to that of finishing the race, then Paul may conceive the fighting as essentially the guarding of a sacred treasure.

For his spiritual warfare, the servant of Christ needs weapons of righteousness on the right hand and on the left. He must be clothed with the whole armour of God – which is at every point a spiritual accoutrement. He must resist the temptation to fight with unworthy weapons or to imitate the strategy of unscrupulous men, for the warfare he wages is not "worldly", and the weapons are not "carnal", though they are powerful enough for the destroying of strongholds. It is all too easy, in winning the battle, to betray the principles for which you began to fight.

If the whole notion of a militant ministry – a salvation "army" – sounds strange and childish now, that is only a symptom of the sentimentalising of the gospel that has invaded all Christian teaching and enervated all Christian work in our easy-going time.

Guardianship of a sacred trust suggests another unfamiliar Pauline metaphor for the Christian minister: he is the earthen vessel wherein is deposited precious treasure. The riches of the gospel is a favorite theme of Paul: the unsearchable riches of Christ, the immeasurable riches of His grace, the glorious riches of the mystery of Christ, the inexpressible gift of God. He writes, too, of the riches of God's wisdom, the riches of His glory, the riches of His goodness, and twice declares that in everything we are enriched in Christ.

We must not discount this language as merely homiletic

exaggeration. Paul would indeed contend that Christ immeasurably enriched human life, that Christians are filled with all the fulness of God. All things are ours; Christ unlocks to us every treasure; the world's bounty and beauty He reveals as the Father's gifts. He clothes life with meaning, robs death of its dread, fills yesterday with peace, today with victory, tomorrow with hope, and subdues all things to serve our good. This is the treasure offered in the gospel, and Christ's servants are "stewards of the mysteries", charged with the safe-keeping and bountiful distribution of the wealth of Christ.

Paul declares that it is required of stewards that they be found faithful, and immediately the whole metaphor – of the treasure of Christian life entrusted to the Lord's stewards – recalls the parable of the "talents" and the charge of Jesus to be faithful. In the same vein, Paul speaks of himself, rather unexpectedly, as approved by God to be entrusted with the gospel, entrusted with preaching by the command of God, and entrusted with a commission. To be in Christ's service is to be trusted with precious things, that could be squandered, or buried in a napkin.

In Paul's reflections upon this idea, the entrusted treasure becomes contrasted with the weakness and worthlessness of the bearer, the steward, the vessel in which the treasure lies. As ministers, having ourselves nothing, we yet, having Christ, possess all things. "We have this treasure in earthen vessels, to show that the transcendent power belongs to God and not to us." And the earthen vessel is elsewhere in scripture worthless, frail, easily broken, sometimes cast away. Once at least it is hidden in a field, and that may also be implied in Christ's parable of the hid treasure The value and validity of the work lie in the truth we bear, and not in the personality through which it finds expression. The life-enrichment we offer men is certainly not our own.

The minister of Christ is, again, an ambassador, an envoy, through whom God makes His appeal to a world alienated from Him. Ambassadorship may appear to be outwardly a position of dignity, rank, and social position, but this is not its meaning: essentially it is one of regal and representative responsibility, and so of representative authority. His message, the best any envoy can bring, of peace and reconciliation, is reliable and effective because he speaks not for himself. And when, "against all the most sacred and inviolable laws of nations" (as Bengel and Theophylact say) the ambassador is placed "in bonds" – and Paul so describes himself – then both dignity and authority are outraged, and insult is offered not only to the man but to the Throne he represents.

Nor is this all. Behind this metaphor for Christian service lies a truth even more bold than that of royal representation. Paul here makes the "proclaiming" of reconciliation a part of the total process by which the world is brought back to God. In the sentence, "God was in Christ reconciling the world to himself . . . and entrusting to us the message of reconciliation" two parts of the reconciling work are set side by side: that which God accomplished in Christ, and that which, so accomplished, is now proclaimed in order to be made effectual. If those to whom the message of peace is entrusted wholly fail, so that the reconciling word never reaches the "enemy", reconciliation will never take place.

This might seem to imply an exaggerated view of the place of preaching in world-salvation, but it is confirmed in Paul's letter to the Romans. The apostle firmly believed that the world would be saved only by the gospel; that to be saved they must believe it, and to believe it they must hear it; "and how are they to hear it without a preacher?" So in another part of the Corinthian correspondence he can say, "It pleased God through the folly of what we preach to save those that believe." In this light the "ambassador" metaphor is not at all too daring; the Christian apostle, missionary, pastor, teacher, evangelist, parent and friend becomes the bearer of the operative, authoritative word by which the world must be saved. The worker represents the Throne – and the throne is one of grace.

Even so, probably the most penetrating, perhaps the most startling, of all Paul's figures for the ministry of Christ's cause, is that of parenthood. Here, the worker is not the bearer of truth, so much as the bearer of spiritual life itself. So Paul can speak of the Galatians as those "with whom I am again in travail". He calls Timothy "my son, who has served as a son with a father", and speaks of Onesimus as "my child, whose father I have become in my imprisonment." We recall, too, his description of his care of the Thessalonians as like that of a nurse for her children.

To make the meaning perfectly clear, he admonishes the Corinthians as beloved children, reminding them that though they may have countless educators in Christ, they did *not* have many fathers – "for I became your father in Jesus Christ through the gospel." This is not to disparage a teaching ministry, but to remind that to impart life is infinitely more privileged, in the final analysis, than to impart information or counsel – and the ultimate goal of all Christian work. Spiritual childlessness, the inability to lead others to the point of decision, to make the heart melt and the new life begin, is not to be lightly accepted or condoned. Christ's servants must learn, with Paul, to travail for souls, and keep awake the expectation that hearts will be born again where the work is faithfully sustained.

The remaining metaphor is the most moving of all. The ministry of all Christ's workers is a double gift. When Christ ascended on high and led captive many prisoners, and in the hour of His glorious triumph distributed gifts to men, that they might share His joy, His royal gifts to the Church He loved were – the ministry: "His gifts were that some should be apostles, some prophets, some evangelists, some pastors and teachers . . ." That is a breath-taking conception, which should lift the heart of every Christian minister, missionary, and other worker, in gratitude to God. Yet there is another side to the truth: for service, and ministry of all kinds, is His gift also to *us*. Says Paul in the same Ephesian letter, "To me, though I am the very least of all the saints, this grace was given, to preach . . ."

It is hard to keep that feeling about Christian work: it is Christ's personal gift to the worker, thus to be used. It is wholly undeserved – "this grace" – we are never good enough for it and never will be. To give up, unless you must, is to throw the gift of a place in His team back in the face of the Giver – and is unthinkable. Men in Christ's service are His gift to the Church, and to be in His service at all is His gift to us: what more could Paul say about "this ministry?"

So enshrined in Paul's allusions and figures is a heart-warming conception of the work to which Christ's servants are called, a conception each does well to retain in memory and return to again and again amid pressures and disappointments, failures and success. We are labourers with Christ in the agelong harvest fields of God. We are builders together with God of the slowly emerging Temple, rising through the centuries, the truly consecrated shrine of dedicated hearts in which God dwells. We are soldiers in the divine war, stewards and vessels bearing eternal riches, ambassadors representing the throne set in the heavens. We are imparters of divine life by the word and the Spirit. We are recipients of the gift of serving, and ourselves the gift of the ascended Lord to the Church for which He gave Himself!

Who calls Thy glorious service hard?
Who deems it not its own reward?

Descriptions

Such being, in Paul's mind, the varied dignity conferred upon Christ's servants by their privilege of serving, it is not surprising that his descriptions of the service itself should suggest a similar variety and high importance; to look a little more closely at phrases already recalled is to realise the dimensions of Christian ministry as Paul conceived it.

Thus, Paul does use the phrase "ministry of reconciliation", meaning more than the "message of reconciliation" of newer translations: for the service of Christ includes the diligent and patient promotion of all that serves the cause of unity and peace on every level and in every realm. In Paul's thought, the reconciliation of man to God is the crucial act by which all the diverse and conflicting forces within man's own personality, within human society, and within God's universe, are finally to be reduced to harmony. This is God's ultimate goal, and Christ's supreme glory: "through him to reconcile to himself all things, whether on earth or in heaven, making peace by the blood of his cross."

A soul at peace with God finds *all* life fall into pattern. It is reconciled to itself, its handicaps, its background, its limitations; it is reconciled to its experience, of adversity, or disappointment, or labour, or obscurity; it is reconciled to others, as brethren in Christ or brethren still to be won. And this total unification of life is achieved by that same act of integration by which the soul is brought to its ordained centre and rest in God. It is of this *total* reconciliation — a purpose so extremely relevant to many sides of modern life — that Paul holds the servant of Christ to be an agent.

Whether in counseling a divided soul, or in healing a neighbourhood feud, in salvaging a breaking marriage, or re-uniting an embittered family, in disciplining a quarreling Church, or in preaching the duty and the arts of peace in industry, in civic affairs, or in inter-racial and inter-national issues, the servant of Christ has a vested interest in peace-making. He is committed, on all questions, to the over-riding divine purpose of reconciliation. That is the psychological and social dimension of his ministry in a divided world.

In sharpest contrast to the unpredictable whims of amoral pagan gods and goddesses, the God of Hebrew faith was righteous: as the Judge of all the earth He could be implicitly relied upon to do that which was right. Righteousness, it follows, was the goal of all His gracious dealing with men, and the deepest purpose behind both the Law and the ministry of the prophets was the reflection of that divine righteousness in all Israel's conduct, relationships, and social life.

Paul knew from his Old Testament that permanent reconciliation depends upon righteousness: "the work of righteousness shall be peace; and the effect of righteousness quietness and confidence for ever." He knew, no less clearly, from his Lord that life in the kingdom of God demands a standard of righteousness exceeding that of the scribes and Pharisees. For him, therefore, the service of Christ must include a "ministry of righteousness".

In practice, the continuing life of the Church, with its public services of worship, its redemptive fellowship, its treasured memories of the ideal incarnate in Jesus, its means of grace, its examples of family life and personal piety, and its continual exposition of moral principles, is the main social agency, aided by the Christian school, for maintaining moral standards of behaviour and of thought in the Western world. More than either the Church or the world sometimes realises, the Christian Church remains keeper of the conscience of Western society, and the ministry of Christ's Church is the appointed leadership of that moral influence by which even yet Christians exercise their calling as lights in the world and the salt of the earth.

The phrase "ministers of a new covenant" had especial significance for Jewish ears. The idea of a divine covenant, or "arrangement", regulating relationships between God and man upon terms which God proposes and man either accepts or rejects, underlay all Old Testament religion. Kings, priests and prophets were in different ways "ministers" of this covenant, making known its terms in each generation and striving to ensure its fulfilment by God's people. When the "old" covenant of Mosaic Law failed to save Israel from Babylonian exile, a "new" covenant was promised, based no longer upon external commandment but upon internal disposition, itself the result of regeneration of the nation by God's own Spirit. This "new" covenant Jesus inaugurated at the Last Supper, and of it Paul conceives all Christ's servants to be "ministers".

This rich background of meaning illumines the historic and theological importance which Paul attaches to Christian ministry. To stand in the succession of the prophets that were before us, as agents of the divine will for man, servants of the divine "dispensation" under which alone man could find blessing, seemed to the apostle the highest work any soul could aspire to do. The covenantal context of Christian service provides its historic and theological dimension, as means established by God for the fulfilment of His promises toward His human family.

And the "experiential" dimension of Christian service is suggested in the phrase "ministry of the Spirit" – which again, Paul does use, despite the modern translations' disguising of it. This is implied, in any case, by the new covenant's replacement of a written code by a regenerate disposition. As the old Law could only expose and condemn breaches of God's will, so its "ministers" were ministers of condemnation – kings exercising justice in God's name, priests offering sacrifices in atonement for disobedience, scribes expounding the Law's demands and warning of judgement. But the typical minister of the new covenant was the preacher of good news, the herald of new life, not of death, and the agent and bearer of the Spirit of the living God.

To be such an agent of the living Spirit is to touch men at the centres of experience, to proclaim and witness again and again the regeneration of human nature. It is to know that God still acts within the soul, and within society – that earthquake, wind and fire are not more potent than the voice of gentle stillness which haunts a soul to whom divine truth has been spoken in the Spirit's power. It is to feel sometimes the pulse of divine energies that kindle and bless others – often when you know that you yourself least deserve to be so used! It is to realise often and again that the ministry of Christ is – the ministry *of Christ*.

In the psychological and social dimension, a ministry of reconciliation; in the ethical and moral dimension, a ministry of righteousness; in the religious dimension, a ministry of God's covenant with men; in the dimension of salvation and of life, a ministry of the Spirit. So Paul thought of the service of Christ; and so should we.

16 *So We Preach*

ROME WAS MAGNIFICENT, luxurious, proud, and above all powerful, the metropolis of the world. Paul had preached his message in Athens, the world's acknowledged intellectual centre, in Ephesus, accepted widely if not universally as the world-centre of culture and beauty, and in Jerusalem, whose claim to importance in matters of religion was unrivalled. As his thoughts turn westward, Paul writes to the Romans of his desire to preach also in their great city, to announce the good news of the kingdom of God at the controlling centre of man's greatest empire.

A visit to the mistress city might have been expected much earlier in Paul's career, and lest it be foolishly suspected that some misgiving or hesitation about Rome's surfeit of religions, philosophies, and "ideologies" had caused the delay, Paul emphatically declares, "I am not ashamed of the gospel . . ." As his fuller exposition of his message in the Roman epistle shows, he believed intensely that his message was reasonable, worthy the attention of intelligent men; and that it was relevant, both to the moral corruption and to the mental confusion of the age; but most of all he believed it had regenerating power. The gospel of Christ was the power of God unto salvation: and Rome, the very symbol and embodiment of worldly power, might be expected to appreciate that argument.

For despite all her philosophical and ethical systems, her brilliant law and experienced statecraft, Rome yet lacked the moral dynamic to clean up the ghettos, the slums and the seaports of her empire, to end the cruelty of her amphitheatres, the disgrace of her slave system. But Paul believed he knew such a dynamic, as he believed he had the secret that could cleanse the moral cesspool of the Mediterranean at Corinth – namely, "Christ crucified, the power of God".

What then was this gospel, this power-laden message, of which Paul boasted? The question is so important, and the adequacy of the answer depends so much upon correct emphasis and true context of ideas, that it is profitable to assemble patiently the various references to the content of Paul's preaching before attempting an analysis.

Evidence

To begin where Paul began, immediately after his conversion he was with the disciples at Damascus, and in the synagogues immediately he proclaimed Jesus, saying, "He is the Son of God." The first extended account of Paul's preaching is the sermon at Pisidian Antioch: here Paul rehearses the calling of Israel and the story of Saul and David – of whom came Jesus; a brief glance at the now-famous John of Jordan, and then twelve verses given to the story of Jesus, His rejection, death, and resurrection, followed by five verses offering forgiveness and deliverance through this Man.

At Iconium Paul speaks boldly "for the Lord"; at Philippi the sum of his message is "Believe in the Lord – Jesus– and you will be saved". At Thessalonica his word is, "This Jesus, whom I proclaim to you, is the Christ." At Athens Paul preached Jesus and the resurrection, so concentrating on these two themes as to suggest twin deities of a new religion! At Corinth, Paul "was occupied with preaching", that is, "testifying to the Jews that the Christ was Jesus."

The exorcists at Ephesus used the revealing incantation, "I adjure you by the Jesus whom Paul preaches", and at Miletus a little later Paul himself recalls his message to that great city in the terms "testifying both to Jews and to Greeks of repentance to God and of faith in our Lord Jesus Christ."

The governor Festus explained to Agrippa the dispute that had arisen about Paul as something concerning the Jews' own superstition, "and about one Jesus, who was dead, but whom Paul asserted to be alive". Paul's own account of the commission given to him, as he describes it to Agrippa, is to witness to the living Christ whom he had seen, to preach forgiveness and repentance, and to testify "both to small and great . . . that the Christ must suffer, and that, by being the first to rise from the dead, he would proclaim light both to the people and to the Gentiles."

Luke's final glimpse of Paul in Rome shows him confronting first the Jews, "testifying to the kingdom of God and trying to convince them about Jesus . . .", and then welcoming to his lodging all who came, Jews and Gentiles, "preaching the kingdom of God and teaching about the Lord Jesus Christ quite openly and unhindered."

So far, Luke's record of the things Paul preached about: turning to Paul's own account, we find in the letter to the Romans that "the word of faith which we preach" is defined at once as leading to the confession that Jesus is Lord and that God raised Him from the dead. In the Corinthian letters, Paul declares, "We preach Christ crucified", and recalls that "When I came to you, brethren, . . . I decided to know nothing among you except Jesus Christ and him crucified." Later, "We preach . . . Jesus Christ as Lord"; and again, "the Son of God, Jesus Christ, whom we preached among you, Silvanus and Timothy and I . . ."; and yet again, "If some one comes and preaches another Jesus than the one we preached . . ."

To the Galatians the apostle writes "[God] was pleased to reveal his Son to me, in order that I might preach him . . ." and to the Ephesians he says, "To me . . . this grace was given, to preach to the Gentiles the unsearchable riches of Christ." When, for the Colossians, he refers to "Christ in you, the hope of glory", Paul cannot forbear to add, "Him we proclaim . . ." And to the Philippians he sends the moving words: "What has happened to me has really served to advance the gospel" (that is to say) "it has become known throughout the whole praetorian guard and to all the rest that my imprisonment is for Christ; and most of the brethren . . . are much more bold to speak the word of God without fear. Some indeed preach Christ from envy and rivalry, but others from good will . . . the former proclaim Christ out of partisanship . . . What then? Only that in every way, whether in pretense or in truth, Christ is proclaimed; and in that I rejoice."

So Paul ends, so far as the New Testament is concerned, exactly as he began in the synagogues of Damascus, rejoicing to proclaim Christ. Repentance, the kingdom, forgiveness, but all centering in Christ, crucified and risen — that is Paul's message. The point is not that in all these references the theme is the same, but that these are all the references there are! *Every time* Paul's preaching is mentioned, this is the content indicated. Paul had nothing else to say to the Roman world, or to the Jewish, but Christ.

Analysis

Paul preached Jesus – risen. Seven times in the above summary the resurrection of Christ is referred to, and the Athenians join Festus in isolating this emphasis as characteristic of Paul's message. "For this hope I am accused by Jews, O king!" says Paul to Agrippa. "Why is it thought incredible by any of you that God raises the dead?" So central to Paul's gospel was the fact that Jesus had risen, that he could say, "If Christ has not been raised, then our preaching is in vain . . . We are even found to be misrepresenting God."

The resurrection assumes of course the crucifixion, and there is no contradiction between this theme of Christ, the hope of glory, and the determination to know nothing save Christ crucified. That Jesus had lived and died was in itself no gospel – for Paul's contemporaries it was scarcely even news – until the personal witness of the apostles to His resurrection raised the question who He was. Once it was established that Jesus was "designated Son of God in power . . . by his resurrection from the dead", the explanation of His death became all important; and it was seen that He "was put to death for our trespasses and raised for our justification". As in Peter's Pentecost sermon – and as indeed in the experience of the Eleven – it is the resurrection that irradiates the cross, and eclipses the tragedy of Calvary with the saving triumph of life eternal.

So it had been in Paul's experience, too. He met the living Christ on the Damascus Road; possibly he had glimpsed the truth in Stephen's rapt gaze upon the risen Christ standing at God's right hand. He saw everything that had gone before – "Christ from a human point of view" – transfigured in resurrection light, and he could not but preach Jesus in an eternal dimension; to use the terms familiar in modern Christian thought, he presented Christ in an eschatological frame of reference.

The ugly phrase is useful, because it denotes two things at once. It stresses that Christ belongs now to the sphere of the *last* things: the risen Jesus is the answer to man's mortality, the divine antidote to all human fear of death's final frustration of man's hopes and aspiration. In Him all that the human heart worthily lives for and lives by is guaranteed against destruction. In Paul's day, fear of the demon world, and after that the Dark, found its resolution in the message of Jesus risen and alive: in our day the same saving word is the divine answer to our dread of the mushroom cloud and the incandescent rain. He is the First and the Last, and the Living One – Jesus risen, the Arbiter and End of human destiny.

But He is the "eschatological" Christ in another sense too, as One not belonging to this world, not another item in the unbroken chain of material – or psychological – cause and effect which binds all earthly things in firm necessity. He is of another order, coming from beyond time into time, "eschatological" in its sense of inbreaking into history from beyond history. He is divine, neither produced by human forces nor subject to man's limitations – He is risen! Man's one sure contact with an ultimate world and an eternal meaning: the living Christ is man's only real clue to what the material world is all about!

Paul preached Jesus – Lord. From Caesarea Philippi onwards this was the crucial point about Jesus – who was He? Son of David, Son of God, Christ, Lord, the precise phrasing of the answer is determined by Jewish or Gentile background, messianic or philosophic implications, but the ascription of divinity and dominance is always clear. Everything professedly Christian – belief, behaviour, Church membership, worship, baptism, true doctrine, the genuineness of the Spirit – is in the New Testament tested by this acknowledgement, that Jesus is Christ, the Son, the Lord of all.

These titles recur eleven times in our summary of references to Paul's preaching; for this confession Paul strove as he presented the story – confession with the lips that Jesus is Lord, because "every one who calls upon the name of the Lord will be saved." "We preach Jesus . . . as Lord; . . . proving that Jesus is the Christ": perhaps it is not surprising that Gallio in Corinth dismissed the whole evangelistic enterprise as "a matter of questions about words and names" – with more insight than he knew. But what names! – for "Lord" was Caesar's title, the slave-owner's title, the pagan's title for their gods many and lords many, and the Jewish title for Jehovah in the Septuagint and in common speech. All this wealth of meaning lay in saying Jesus is Lord: a matter of names indeed!

On Paul's lips the title "Lord" possessed both messianic and moralist implications. At Thessalonica, for preaching Jesus as Lord he is accused of turning the world upside down, acting against the decrees of Caesar, and saying there is another king, Jesus. At Ephesus he argued and pleaded about the kingdom of God, and at Rome, again, this aspect of his teaching is twice mentioned by Luke. It must be remembered that at this time "kingdom of God" was still a fresh and living phrase, not yet an omnibus expression for all Christendom, all Christian experience, thought and work. It still meant the reign of God within the heart, through Christ, accepted as life's Lord. It signified the prophetic and apocalyptic hope of the Day of the Lord, when God should have His way, as that had been moralised in the teaching of John and Jesus.

So preaching Jesus as Lord was essentially a demand for moral surrender to the reign of Christ. It was an assertion of Christian values and standards, of the kingdom of Christian ends. It is preaching Jesus – again – but now in His ethical relevance, rather than eschatological: preaching His standards, challenges, disciplines, invitations, reign and judgement. It meant really making Him Lord in citizenship, in politics, in human relations, in the domestic circle, in daily work, and in the heart.

Paul preached Jesus – Judge. At Athens the sermon reached its climax in the declaration: "The times of ignorance God overlooked, but now he commands all men everywhere to repent, because he has fixed a day on which he will judge the world in righteousness by a man whom he has appointed, and of this he has given assurance to all men by raising him from the dead." The "man" here is a Gentile equivalent of "the Son of Man" of Jewish prophecy and of the synoptic story. To Agrippa, and to the Ephesian elders, Paul recalls the emphasis he had laid upon repentance toward God, and this, too, implies the divine judgment upon human conduct.

With what effect Paul could preach on this aspect of his theme, the episode before Felix eloquently testifies. It is true that he had a vulnerable target: Felix, says Foakes-Jackson, on the evidence of Josephus, Tacitus and Suetonius alike, was "one of the worst of men". Tacitus said that he exercised royal power with the disposition of a slave. Drusilla, sitting beside him as Paul preached, was his third wife, recently persuaded to desert her husband to join him – some would argue that Luke means he has just arrived from getting her! In any case Paul's choice of subject was a bold one, for Felix was a Roman, an official, and an aristocrat: yet when he sent for Paul to hear him speak, Paul "argued about justice, and self-control, and future judgement!" Felix, not unnaturally, was "alarmed" (not merely annoyed), and cried out, "Go away . . ."

Not often in these days is Christ preached with that effect. This is, again in useful modern phrase, presenting Christ in existential terms, as demanding a response here and now, personally and crucially. It is preaching to a crisis of decision; a confrontation now, "in personal existence" and not merely in ideas, of the hearer and God in judgement. It is the presentation of truth directly and insistently, in the realism of personal encounter, as at once gracious opportunity, ultimate demand, and final threat. For whatever we may decide, in our feeble freedom of opinion, to do about the gospel, Jesus remains – and remains to judge.

Such are the notes Paul felt his time demanded, and in so far as our time resembles his, such are the notes that once more must be sounded. A down-curving age of spiritual declension creates urgent moral anxieties, about the welfare of the young, about the drift of the world towards disaster, about the pressing dilemmas of crime and punishment, of science without moral direction, of a world apparently headed for technologically perfect suicide. If in these circumstances we have anything to say of moral relevance and power, the world will listen, when it is long tired of our theologies and our denunciations. And we have: in the living Christ is a pattern of moral excellence and a dynamic for moral achievement which hold the answer the heart of man is seeking. We must preach Christ, as living and as Lord, to follow, to obey, to surrender to, to die for – as He died for us.

In the intellectual and moral difficulties of communication, too, when our assumptions and our terminology jar upon the modern mind, the portrait of Jesus does not. True, to present Jesus clearly demands the best of scholarship, historical insight, a delicate sense of truth, ethical penetration, appreciation, depth, and vision: but if we confront men and women with Him they will understand. He is still the magnet of the heart; like the Greeks in Jerusalem of old, there are many modern men who cry, We would see Jesus.

And what better can we do when men assail the divided, weakened Church, than show them Christ? One cannot imagine Paul pressing the claims of the Church upon outsiders: "We preach not ourselves, but Christ Jesus the Lord . . ." is still the determinative principle of evangelism. The Church may let men down; He never will. If we would learn of Paul to present Jesus in eternal reference, in ethical relevance, in existential realism of demand, we have a theme vast, and inexhaustible, and immensely powerful still. For He is even yet Christ the power of God, and the wisdom of God, the final truth and everlasting Judge.

17 *His Letters Are Weighty*

"I WOULD NOT seem to be frightening you with letters. For they say, 'His letters are weighty and strong . . !'" This seems to be our only evidence of the reactions evoked by Paul's correspondence. Galatia would have agreed that his letters were "strong"; Rome would certainly echo "weighty"; Philippi and Colosse and Thessalonia might have felt that more personal comments were more appropriate to the writings they received, so vividly recalling the presence and personality of their beloved leader.

Our own reaction is usually different again: "difficult, contentious, involved, discursive" — especially if we struggle with archaic English only half-translating impetuous Greek! If we remember what nourishment of faith and love these pages have brought to us, we might well add "how varied, and rich, and instructive, and compelling, and heart-warming and true!" Or recalling their influence upon the Church, their creative force in Christian society, their role in shaping the philosophical and political thought of the Western world, we might be constrained to marvel that so few words, so hastily and "accidentally" penned, could have enshrined such intensity of thought and spiritual power.

For granted that behind the human circumstances lay divine providence, and behind the apostolic counselling a divine inspiration, it remains true that Paul's letters were never intended for posterity. They are "occasional papers" called forth by contemporary situations; they served to give clarity and permanence to truths already orally taught during hasty visits, to answer questions about faith or conduct, to exchange news of Churches or colleagues, to appeal for help or give thanks for help received, to prepare for visits or explain absence, to encourage, exhort, advise, correct, or rebuke. Not one letter sets forth the whole of Paul's teaching, even on one subject, in any systematic and balanced fashion. Just because he was always the eager pastor-teacher-evangelist, concerned with people and never with academic questions, we with our historical and theological interests have to piece together his utterances, comparing one with another and allowing for local circumstances and immediate practical needs.

Nevertheless these partial and occasional writings have een treasured through twenty centuries as a supreme expression of the Christian spirit; as an irreplaceable interpreation of Jesus; as a canon or standard by which the teaching f the Church in every generation has been tested and eformed; as an armoury from which has been drawn weapons o fight heresy after heresy; as a burning bush at which nnumerable torches have been kindled; as an unfailing pring of spiritual refreshment and intellectual power.

Paul's are the earliest pages of our New Testament, and vere intended for reading aloud in meetings of the Churches ddressed. Sometimes, even in his own lifetime, copies circuated among local Churches: he asks that the Colossian etter be read at Laodicea, and one sent to Laodicea be read n exchange at Colosse. The absence, from some copies, f the address "to Rome", "to Ephesus", suggests that some ditions of these letters passed freely over wider areas. The impulse to collect various letters would be much tronger after Paul's death, when the passing of the apostolic ge made every memory and utterance of the first leaders loubly precious, and different Churches assembled little libraries" of Pauline correspondence.

Already in the second epistle of Peter there is reference o the letters which "our beloved brother Paul wrote to you ccording to the wisdom given him, speaking [of the last hings] as he does in all his letters. There are some things n them hard to understand, which the ignorant and unstable wist to their own destruction, as they do the other scripures." Thus to set Paul's writing beside "the other scriptures" s the very highest tribute any Christian could pay to Paul's uthority, wisdom, and inspiration.

The phrase "in all his letters" and the reference to a letter from Laodicea" remind us that we have not everything Paul wrote. Allusions in the existing epistles to the Corinhians confirm this: in our "first epistle" he says "I wrote o you in a letter not to associate with immoral men", and n our "second" letter he mentions one written "out of nuch affliction and anguish of heart and with many tears" hat made them sorry and which he also for a time regretted vriting. This hardly describes our "first Corinthians", and t is perhaps not surprising that it did not survive: it may have been the one that "frightened" them! How many others, of purely local and temporary importance, also perished, we cannot know; sometimes we wonder if paragraphs which sit awkwardly in the existing letters (2 Corinthians 6:14 to 7:1, for example, and Philippians 3:1 to 4:1) may not be fragments from this lost correspondence.

Priority in time is disputed between the letters sent to Thessalonica and that written for the group of Churches in Galatia. These Gentile Churches in Lystra, Derbe, Iconium and neighbouring towns were firstfruits of Paul's missionary enterprise, and dear to his heart; but they were also the living evidence of his universalistic gospel. A narrower, Judaist view of Christianity had been preached among them, demanding Jewish observances as necessary to salvation, and impugning Paul's apostolic status and authority as an exponent of the gospel. Unable at once to revisit these Churches, Paul sent off this short and vehement letter, countering the Judaist distortions of the gospel and recalling the Galatian converts to their first faith and experience.

Paul necessarily asserts his own direct call of God to the apostleship, that the Galatians may be reassured about their faith, and pleads that Christian liberty and fruitful life under the rule of the Spirit (and not the Jewish Law) shall be maintained – not sacrificed for a futile return to Jewish legalism. The letter shows Paul at his most impassioned and controversial, because the issues were exceptionally important and his concern for these unsettled and confused young converts very great. Yet amid the serious arguments precious passages occur, especially the intimate glimpses of Paul's inner life, and his beautiful description of the harvest of the Spirit.

Paul remembered vividly, from his visit to Thessalonica in Macedonia, how readily and completely his converts there had turned from idols to the living God. But he received news (possibly through Timothy and Silas when they rejoined him at Corinth) that the Thessalonian Christians were showing unusual excitement about the second coming of Christ, though some were troubled at the passing of Christian friends before that great event. Paul sends calm and reassuring instruction that all Christians living and dead shall share Christ's final victory, and at the same time urges those who look earnestly for that Day to behave as vigilant, disciplined, and sober-minded "children of the Day". They must follow faithfully the calm and busy example given them by the apostles and not neglect their daily duties for apocalyptic thrills. The letter is a gem of Paul's simpler, unhurried style.

A second letter followed, however, more official and severe, and even "frigid" in tone. It appears that advent excitement had grown; some declared the last events had already begun, and continued to neglect daily Christian obligations, even to their families. Paul instructs them about preparatory signs that must herald Christ's coming, and sternly counsels the enthusiasts to mind their Christian business.

The Church at Corinth sent to Paul a number of questions concerning faith and conduct, by the hands of "Chloe's people", apparently the Stephanas, Fortunatus, and Achaicus whose arrival Paul welcomes and whose character he commends. They brought also news of the Church's welfare, which was of a less welcome kind. Paul's reply is our "first" epistle to the Corinthians, in which he first chides their partisanship, which is dividing the Church into parties following Peter, or Apollos, or claiming to follow himself, or Christ. He reminds them that their faith stands not in human teaching or teachers, but in the word of God, and that all are fellow-workers in God's fields. He rebukes severely a case of gross immorality within the Church, and also a tendency to go to law against fellow Christians.

On the matters which their letter had raised, Paul discusses the Christian attitude to marriage, and the principles which must guide Christians whether to eat, or to abstain from, meats slaughtered as offerings in idol temples. Some question of theirs about his apostolic authority receives firm reply, and he adds warning against a somewhat lax attitude towards worldly temptations. He advises, too, on the conduct of women in the Church assemblies, lest offence be given to outsiders.

Disorder attending the conduct of the Lord's Supper is then dealt with, leading to discussion of a general divisiveness and want of dignity in the Corinthians' worship, due to over-valuing of ecstatic spiritual "gifts". Paul rebukes the self-assertiveness that sets one "gift" against another, and insists that all gifts are manifestations of one Spirit, bestowed for the common good of the one Body of Christ, and all profitless unless exercised in love – which leads to the glorious chapter on love's pre-eminence, power, and permanence. Thence Paul passes to his great defence of Christian belief in the resurrection of the body, and instructions concerning the collection for Judea's poorer Churches close a long and priceless letter.

The "second" letter to Corinth reviews, in a spirit of reconciliation and thanksgiving, the recent troubled relationship between Paul and the Church, and passes to an exposition of the place and glory, the motives and aims, of the apostolic ministry, and its costliness and triumphs. An elaboration of the appeal for the Judean Churches provides an exposition of the principles of Christian stewardship. Then an unexpected change of mood fills the last three chapters with self-defence, remonstrance, rebuke, warning to the recalcitrant – almost as though these chapters belong to the earlier "severe" letter, though they may be intended rather for the stubborn, unreconciled minority. In these two letters we sense still the pastoral care and wisdom which directed Paul's ministry, and his awareness that high ideals must be translated into codes of behaviour in the real world. Probably in no other of his writings is the step from loftiest doctrine to lowliest duty made to appear so logical, and so natural.

The best known, and historically the most important, of Paul's letters is that to the Church at Rome. Its purpose was simple: to introduce Paul to a Church which did not know him personally, so preparing his way for a visit to Rome on the journey he meant to take to Spain. The introduction, however, was complicated by his desire to "be sped on my journey there by you" – a tactful request for support for a new westward mission – and also by unfavourable rumours about Paul which had already reached Rome.

These related principally to misunderstandings of his gospel of the free, unmerited grace of God towards sinners of every race — which seemed to some both ethically dangerous and a denial of Jewish prerogatives. Possibly, too, Rome had heard strange things of his repeated clashes with authority, and wondered at the civic results of his moral teaching.

So the "introduction" becomes a defensive statement of Paul's doctrine of salvation. The world is indeed under divine judgement, as its moral state reveals, and in this Jews share no less than Gentiles: all are guilty. But God has set forth Christ as a sacrifice for sin, on condition that men shall believe: faith is the unvarying condition of divine favour under the old covenant and under the new. Thus a parallel can be drawn between man's sinful, mortal state through Adam's sinfulness, and his saved, immortal state through Christ's redemptive righteousness, if man has faith.

To suggest that salvation by faith, instead of by moral effort to fulfil the Law, justifies a careless continuance in sin, totally misunderstands what faith is. For faith unites a man to Christ in death to sin, and the new Spirit of life in Christ transforms him completely. The wonderful eighth chapter of this letter describes Christian life in the Spirit of Christ as no other passage in literature has ever done.

But just when we expect Paul to apply his great doctrine to practical Christian living, he breaks off to discuss the relation of Jewish privileges to this plan of redemption by universal faith. He does so with such suddenness that it has been suggested that he here incorporates an outline of teaching often given on other occasions. He protests his undying love for his people; he argues that faith, not heredity, determines who are Abraham's true children; he asserts the sovereignty of God, who deals with men as He will; he recalls the stubbornness of Israel against every offer of God's grace, so that they have no complaint; and he affirms his hope that in the end Israel also will be saved.

Then Paul returns to the theme of salvation, to appeal for life consistent with the great mercies of God, a quality of living that shall be manifest in the service of Christ's cause, in responsible Christian citizenship (which he fully expounds), and in a self-sacrificing fellowship of mutual concern with all who believe. An appeal for unity and comradeship concludes the most sustained and powerful of all Paul's invaluable arguments.

A group of four much shorter letters share a prison background, whether the same prison, and where, cannot be dogmatically stated, though the Roman captivity seems most probable. The shortest, and most intimate, is to a friend, Philemon, his wife Apphia, and the minister of the Church meeting in their house, Archippus; it is a moving appeal for kindly welcome and forgiveness for Philemon's runaway and thieving slave, Onesimus, now converted and returned to his master by Paul. The note breathes the spirit, and informally defines the principles, by which in time (though too long a time) slavery was banished from Christian lands; it also reveals Paul in a close and tender, almost playful, light we would be loth to have missed.

The letters to Ephesus and to Colosse are so similar that almost simultaneous production seems certain. The Church at Colosse was not of Paul's personal founding, but when it was troubled with strange versions of the gospel, and especially with heretical ideas concerning angel-worship and the demon world, a peculiar amalgam of Judaism, superstition, and Greek speculation, combined with certain practices of doubtful morality, Paul wrote with firmness and great eloquence to assert the fulness of redemption by faith in Christ, the pre-eminence, in all worlds, of Jesus Himself, and the soundness and completeness of the Christian ethic they had already been taught. The argument is everywhere profound and cogent, but Colossians is especially valuable for its wonderful exaltation of Christ.

The Ephesian letter bears more than most the marks of the "secretary" whom Paul regularly employed to pen his correspondence. It has somewhat the character of an "encyclical" celebrating the glories of Christian redemption, the wonder of free grace, the miracle of salvation, the mystery and marvel of the Church in the purposes of God. The unity of Jew and Gentile in one Body, and the endowment of that Body by the risen Lord with the Christian ministry and with life growing steadily towards divine completion, are glowingly described, and a conspectus of Christian life in society and in the home leads to the memorable exhortation to put on the whole armour of God in confident expectation of spiritual conflict — and victory — in all realms. No other letter of Paul's achieves quite the sustained exultation of mood or the intensely packed thought of this epistle; and if sometimes the reader is left breathless, one may suppose that the writer pursuing Paul's headlong dictation must often have felt the same!

The fourth "prison letter", that to the Philippians, is different again in tone, calmer, affectionate, more personal. It is essentially a dignified note of thanks for gifts sent to the apostle, but occasion is taken to assure the readers, first of Paul's own welfare and the good effects, for the gospel's progress in the capital, of his imprisonment; and secondly of the welfare after sickness of their beloved pastor Epaphroditus. At the same time, certain incipient divisions in the Church, due mainly to over-zealous womenfolk and a spirit of rivalry, are set in the light of the self-emptying of Christ, the Servant of God. Rather suddenly, the dangers of Jewish legalism emerge and are thoroughly examined. Both the passage describing Christ's "humiliation" and that revealing the temper of Paul's own spiritual endeavour place this letter among the most precious of all; his words of thanksgiving, when he comes to them, breathe a joy, gratitude, and contentment that all envy but few attain.

If we hesitate to claim the mighty epistle to the Hebrews as one of Paul's letters, it is certainly not because it is unworthy of his genius, nor — equally certainly — because he was incapable of writing it. The real difficulties lie in its language, so like and yet in usage so unlike Paul's; in its unexpected content, so unlike Paul's other letters; in its anonymity, and the apparent betrayal of a second-generation source when it claims that the gospel was "attested unto us by those who heard" Jesus. Nevertheless, Hebrews could not have been written until Paul had wrestled successfully with the extravagant claims of Jewish Christians for the Mosaic Law and the covenant; and it seems probable that whoever wrote it had sat long (at least metaphorically) at Paul's feet.

Similar (but less cogent) doubts attend Paul's authorship of the letters to Timothy and to Titus. Here the language and content, and the difficulty of fitting the letters into the story of Paul's life, conflict so strongly with the generally "Pauline" tone of this detailed counsel to two younger pastors, that a compromise view of their origin is favoured: the three letters as we now have them are said to be reproductions of counsel such as Paul would have given to his lieutenants, here faithfully and lovingly preserved in his name, interspersed with genuine notes jealously guarded and now given permanent and useful publication. This saves for us the favourite passages, where Paul recalls his, or Timothy's, past experience, or where Paul anticipates his death, while allowing us to regard as "secondary" those passages where the thought or spirit seems a little below Paul's usual standard. Perhaps this is too convenient; but dogmatism is unjustified, and certainly as yet unattainable.

All in all, Paul's writings do not bulk large in the New Testament. Even including the "Pastorals", they occupy less than Luke's Gospel and Acts; without the "Pastorals", less than Jeremiah, or Matthew-John. Yet through these pages Paul has taught the whole Church through all the Christian centuries the mind of the Master and the inner truth of the gospel. Paul is deeply concerned that Christians should "in understanding be men"; while acknowledging his obligation to the ignorant and the barbarian, and fully aware of the danger that knowledge "puffs up" where love builds up, Paul is nevertheless impatient of Christians who will not grasp the truth, or perceive the moral implications of their profession, or attain to the full assurance of faith. He would agree with T. R. Glover that Christian discipleship demands the "thought-out" life, and with John Clifford that "God does not want your cleverness – or your ignorance". The open mind is not for Paul an empty mind: he held that a man should know whom he has believed, and why, and to what purpose. His labour of writing has ever this protective, informative, spiritually educational end: as he so frequently said, "I would not have you to be ignorant . . . we have not so learned Christ."

18 *For the Defence of the Gospel*

THE MORE COMPLETELY any man accomplishes his lifework, the less likely it is that his work will be truly valued. The problems he entirely solves will seem no problems at all to those who inherit his solutions; truths once strenuously contended for will appear obvious and incontrovertible within three generations. That is why some effort of historical imagination, and some exposition of forgotten ideas, is unavoidable if a successful man's true stature is to be fully appreciated.

Paul knew himself appointed for the defence of the gospel, not only during his later imprisonment, but in a more important sense throughout his ministry; and he vigorously maintained his intellectual warfare on several fronts at once.

Against Racialism

Luke traces out for us the steps by which the Church was driven, with much hesitation, by persecution and by the pressure of events like the conversion of the Samaritans, of the Eunuch, of Cornelius, and of Gentiles at Antioch, to a slow realisation of her world-wide task. To us the difficulties seem unreal. Had not Jesus said men should come from north, south, east and west; had He not directed the preaching of the gospel in all the world and to all nations; had He not welcomed Samaritan, Roman, Syro-Phenician, publican and outcast?

Yet the guests at the messianic banquet were to sit down with Abraham, Isaac, and Jacob, and in all pious Jewish eyes that implied that they would first be circumcised, accepted within Jewry, and made members of the chosen people. Judaism itself accepted proselytes, provided full assent to Mosaic faith and Law was given by means of baptism, circumcision and sacrifice: the Church surely could not be more lax than Judaism!

This was not merely Jewish prejudice. Scripturally, the promises of salvation were to Israel and not to the world; theologically, Jesus was the Jewish Messiah and not a pagan "saviour" or "divine hero"; legally, the demand for circumcision, separation, and "cleanness" was a divine law, not lightly to be disregarded; ethically, the only safeguard of true godliness that pious hearts knew was the discipline of Judaism; religiously, the scruples about social contact and compromise with heathen ways were wisely founded and supported by unhappy experience; historically, Jesus was Himself a Jew, and so were the Eleven, and the Master had confined His ministry almost entirely to Jews and their half-brothers the Samaritans. Did it not follow from all this that converts from other nations, if they came, must first become good Jewish proselytes, and then as "Jews" accept the Jewish Messiah and His salvation?

Such an interpretation of Christ's intention and the Church's task severely limited evangelistic zeal, multiplied obstacles to conversion, and implied that Christianity would remain, as it had begun, a movement within Judaism, a sect or brotherhood parallel to the Johannine Baptists, the Essenes, the Pharisees, and the communities at Qumran, and never become a world faith, inter-racial and universal. If these consequences make the Judaist arguments seem even less convincing, that is only because Paul so successfully opposed this narrowing of Christian horizons. As Luke makes clear, it was the first Gentile mission journey which precipitated final decision on the question; action, and not argument, defined the issues, and the part of Barnabas and Paul in the discussions of the Council of Jerusalem was simply to recount "what signs and wonders God had done through them."

This is not to say that Paul was content to demand that the Church must accept his Gentile converts because God had done so. He contended that they were already part of Israel – the "new Israel" of God. Paul acknowledged no double status among Christians: Gentiles had been alienated from the commonwealth of Israel and strangers to the covenants of promise, and far off, but now in Christ they have been brought near, and are no longer strangers, but fellow-citizens with the saints, members of the household of God, built upon the same foundation into one holy temple in the Lord. For Christ made Jew and Gentile one, reconciling both to God in one body: "for through him we both have access in one Spirit to the Father."

So Gentiles are "grafted" into the living stock of Israel; the Galatians are blessed as part of the Israel of God; those who were "not my people" become "sons of the living God". There have always been two Israels: one, the physical descendants of Abraham; the other, those who imitate Abraham's faith, his "spiritual children". To share Abraham's faith is to be Abraham's "child"; he is the "father of all who believe", and indeed the "father of many nations". Thus, "if you are Christ's, then you are Abraham's offspring, heirs according to the promise."

"God is not the God of the Jews only, but of the Gentiles also": "there is no distinction between Jew and Greek: the same Lord is Lord of all and bestows His riches upon all who call upon Him." The consequence is boldly drawn – "There is neither Jew nor Greek, . . . neither slave nor free, . . . neither male nor female: for you are all one in Christ Jesus."

In that sentence the attempt to keep Christianity within the narrow bounds of Judaism lies defeated. God chose well a Jew of the Dispersion, a citizen of Rome, with a Christlike passion for souls, to be "apostle of the Gentiles" and interpreter of the limitless purpose of Jesus to the whole world.

Against Legalism

Paul's universalism rests upon the sufficiency of faith alone in Christ to save. "Believe on the Lord Jesus, and you will be saved." The gospel is "the power of God for salvation to every one who has faith"; God offers righteousness "through faith in Jesus Christ for all who believe." Faith is response to the gospel, confessed before men, obedient to the Lord whom it believes, but it remains essentially a personal adherence of trust and submission towards the dying and living Lord Jesus.

Such faith is contrasted, as means of salvation, with keeping the Law – whether the Jewish legal code or the moral law written on Gentile hearts. The Judaist desire to have all Christians bound first to Moses' Law and only thereafter to Christ seemed to Paul to strike at the heart of the free gospel of God's grace. Salvation earned was no free gift: "a man is not reckoned righteous by works of the law but through faith . . . you who would be justified by the law are severed from Christ, fallen away from grace."

Paul's argument appeals partly to precedent: blessing was promised to Abraham before he was circumcised, four hundred years before the law was given: "Abraham *believed God,* and it was reckoned to him as righteousness." So Habakuk defined the principle of the old covenant: "He who through faith is righteous shall live." But Paul appeals also to experience: Law could not save, but only expose, and by prohibition kindle desire. He argues, thirdly, from the principle that sinful man cannot deserve anything good from God: "By grace you have been saved through faith: and this is not your doing, it is the gift of God . . . Now to one who works, his wages are not reckoned as a gift but as his due, and to one who does not work but trusts . . . his faith is reckoned as righteousness . . . If it is by grace, it is no longer on the basis of works: otherwise grace would be no longer grace." And Paul argues, fourthly, from the work which Christ has done: "if you receive circumcision Christ will be of no advantage to you . . . If righteousness were through the law, then Christ died to no purpose."

The permanent issue here is the nature of Christianity as a *gospel* – as good news of salvation offered freely and to all. Throughout Christian history, the attempt has been repeated to rest some part of salvation upon what man can do for himself, so avoiding the humiliation of entire dependence on the favour of God in Christ, and assuaging man's self-esteem. Paul would have none of it. For then salvation would be for those who do not really need it: for the helpless, the desperate, the sinful, and the lost, there would be no hope – if human effort is demanded. If we can save ourselves, then Christ is not the Saviour.

Moreover, if faith alone in Christ is not sufficient – if some righteousness, or faithfulness, or merit in ourselves must be added to make salvation sure – then none can be certain, now, of pardon, acceptance, and peace. We can only hope: and that is *not* the glowing, assured, apostolic faith. The freeness of God's grace, the sufficiency of Christ's redeeming work, hope for the helpless and assurance for all, seemed to Paul essential principles of the gospel, which must stand or fall with the truth that faith in Christ was sufficient to save.

Against Humanism

Beneath this concern for gospel truth lies, however, the deeper jealousy for the unshared efficacy of Christ as Saviour. That Christ should be "of no advantage to you", or that it might be implied "Christ died to no purpose", was to Paul near blasphemy. It was also self-impoverishing: a little, humanistic Christ, conceived as something less than truly divine, shorn by speculative thought or by ill-informed faith, of His unique glory as the only-begotten Son of the ever-living God, meant a limited, under-motived, power-starved religious experience, hardly deserving to be called Christian.

Thus, none will rightly emulate the spirit of Jesus unless he sufficiently appreciates the selfless devotion to others' interests that led Christ to forego equality with God, to "empty himself", and taking the form of a servant to be born in the likeness of men and become obedient even to the death of the cross. To realise who Jesus was is to understand that such self-emptying is the only possible path to glory in Christian eyes.

In the same way, none will rightly apprehend the immense power available in Christ unless he appreciates "the working of [God's] great might which he accomplished in Christ when he raised him from the dead and made him sit at his right hand in the heavenly places, far above all rule and authority and power and dominion . . . and put all things under his feet." From such a conception of Jesus risen, ascended, and victorious, Paul can argue immediately that the Christian, too, has been raised to victory over sin and the demon-world, and should so live.

A maximum faith and a rich experience belong intimately together: so do an adequate conception of Christ and a robust confident hope. Some at Corinth doubted the promise of physical resurrection. With particular difficulties Paul deals briefly, but patiently. He illustrates the change from mortal to immortality by the strange process of identity-through-transformation annually witnessed in the development of the seed-grain through "death" to the "new" mature plant – which is yet the same. He argues that our sharing in Christ's resurrection body is no more strange than our partaking now in Adam's body of "dust". Given the power of God, why should we doubt that we shall all be changed, that death's sting will be drawn, and the grave itself swallowed in victory?

But though Paul offers the Corinthians patient argument, the heart of his great exposition of the Christian hope lies in his conception of Christ, risen, exalted, reigning at God's right hand. Cephas, the Eleven, James, over five hundred, and then Paul himself, had seen the living Lord: so they preached and so the Church believed. This doubted, the practical consequences were serious. Faith and forgiveness are illusions; baptism, as commitment to a living Lord, loses its meaning; endurance of suffering and peril loses its impulse and reward; Christian character loses one compelling motive for self-discipline, the natural reaction to "tomorrow we die" being "eat, drink, be merry!" Apostolic testimony as a whole proves to be false in a material particular, and Christians – whatever they feel – are yet in their sins.

"But in fact Christ has been raised" – the firstfruits and guarantee of the Christian's resurrection. Our hope is sure, if we hold firmly to a full and informed faith in Jesus; and we may remain steadfast, immovable, always abounding in the work of the Lord, well knowing that in the Lord our labour is not in vain.

In the letter to Colosse, intellectual distortions of Christian truth are met with Paul's most emphatic assertions of the uniqueness and glory of Christ, but here again the theological contention has practical purpose, to safeguard the depth and fulness of Christian experience. Details of the "Colossian heresy" are obscure. Something of extreme Jewish scrupulousness about food, drink, festivals, circumcision, the Sabbath, self-abasement and the avoidance of uncleanness, seems to have been combined with speculations akin to theosophy – advanced mystical "knowledge" or "philosophy and empty deceit, according to human tradition, according to the elemental spirits of the universe"; and making much of visions, ecstasies, rigour of devotion and severity to the body, and the worship of angels.

To judge from other "Gnostic" teaching of broadly similar type, this odd assortment of notions and requirements was thought to be necessary because, while Christ could deliver from sin, fulness of salvation from matter itself (conceived as corrupting to everything spiritual) and from the spirit forces under which man's life was held in bondage, needed more than simple faith in Jesus. And this was so because Christ Himself was thought to be but one among many "emanations" of the Godhead – angelic or "spiritual" powers and personalities, friendly or hostile, by overcoming or placating whom man may hope to be saved in the spiritual world, as by asceticism and severity to the body he may be saved from the corruption of the material world.

Paul's reply to this denial of the adequacy of Christ's saving work is the greatest of all his expositions of the unparalleled, ineffable dignity of Christ. Paul identifies Christ with the Reason informing all creation, with the Origin whence all things came to be, with the End towards which all things tend in the ongoing movement of the universe, and with the final Value for the sake of which all things exist. Christ is therefore "the Head of all rule and authority", supreme over all created forces and in all realms. These are astonishing claims, but they merely spell out in detail the common Christian faith in Jesus as the eternal Son of the eternal God.

Moreover, Christ is "Head of the body, the beginning" of all things Christian, too; and "the firstborn from the dead". In Him we have, already, our redemption, both forgiveness and reconciliation; and this was accomplished "in the body of his flesh by his death" – the flesh itself, though material, thus having part in the process of redemption. All this avails only "provided that you continue in the faith . . . not shifting from the hope of the gospel which you heard." For those who so do, Christ is "the image of the invisible God . . . In him all the fulness of God was pleased to dwell . . . [In him] are hid all the treasures of wisdom and knowledge . . . In him the whole fulness of deity dwells bodily, and *you have come to fulness of life* in him."

Christ is "pre-eminent", in creation, in the Church, and in Christian experience, and because He is adequate in nature, unique in glory, the Christian is complete in Him. No need of Law, or theosophy, of ritual calendar, ascetic self-torture, ecstatic visions or angelic intermediaries: faith is sufficient, because Christ is sufficient, and having Him the Christian has all sufficiency in all things.

Paul saw clearly that to reduce Christ to historical and humanistic terms was to impoverish Christianity upon every level – of ethics, of hope, and of spiritual resources: and he strenuously fought against it.

Against Sophistry

To Paul's earnest mind, a salvation so free, a Saviour so glorious, guaranteed in advance the highest moral endeavour by believers; but all were not equally earnest, or clear-sighted, and the perpetual danger of a free salvation offered to faith alone was soon evident in the early Church. If Christ had done all that was needed to save, may not man live as he likes? If grace overflows to sinners, let us sin more that grace may further overflow! A lawless, amoral licentiousness might seem to be an impossible consequence of preaching the power of Christ to save: but the impossible happened, and against it Paul argued with all the force of a conscience outraged, and a love jealous for the honour of Christ.

To all such immoral sophistries Paul's replies are exceptionally vigorous. He repudiates "slanderous" charges, declaring their authors "enemies of the cross of Christ" whose "condemnation was just". He insists upon detailed ethical teaching on the social, sexual, domestic, and civic obligations binding upon all who professed the name of Christ. He warned of judgement on all who do evil, called every disciple to the imitation of Christ, declared that the rule of the Spirit had broken the rule of sin, and though the Law could not save a man it was still "holy and just and good", to be fulfilled "in us, who walk not according to the flesh but according to the Spirit".

But for Paul, all this is already implied in the faith that saves. For faith in Christ is not to be interpreted in merely intellectualist, merely mystical, or merely sacramentalist terms, but as a union of mind and heart and will with Christ, a union so close and so complete that we identify ourselves with His attitude to sin in all its forms. Resting faith upon His work for us at Calvary, we assent to all His cross implies – the divine judgement upon sin as evil, His own resolute opposition to it as alien in His Father's world, its inexcusable malice, cruelty, and viciousness in putting innocence and purity to shameful death. Accepting His cross as our sacrifice for sin we are consenting to die with Him to all sin's allurements and power, and to rise with Him to a life centred upon God and holiness. This is not, for Paul, what faith ought to imply; it is what faith *means*.

To accept Christ as Saviour is to consent to be saved out of sinning. Man cannot be saved by his own moral effort, but to be saved by Christ is nevertheless a moral transformation, and saving faith is a creative energy of goodness that attains a quality, degree and depth of saintliness otherwise inconceivable in sinful hearts.

By that strong contention, Paul saved for Christianity the hard-won fruits of the long battle of the Hebrew prophets for ethical religion; he carried forward into the Church something of the moral rigour of the Jewish Law and the lofty Hebrew conception of the holiness of God; and he preserved for later ages the moral realism of the teaching of Jesus. Thus Paul helped to prevent the glorious gospel of free grace from degenerating into yet another religious mysticism pandering to every fleshly appetite in the name of philosophical or theosophical "liberty", such as abounded in that Graeco-Roman world.

By his insight, advocacy, and example, with penetration, foresight, and unwearying tenacity, Paul stoutly defended the message of Christ from every subtle distortion and persuasive misrepresentation. Repeatedly he warned his young converts against being deluded "with beguiling speech": the time has not yet come when we can safely ignore his far-seeing counsel.

Paul and the Secrets of Power

Assessments and Explanations
Energies Evoked from Within
Power Conferred from Above

19 *Assessments and Explanations*

"ONE OF THE most influential teachers of mankind," is James Stalker's somewhat lukewarm tribute to the apostle Paul. "An exceptional man, the maker of an epoch," is T. R. Glover's more adequate summary. "A great figure in the history of religion" adds C. H. Dodd, and G. B. Caird declares him "By far the greatest figure of his time", quoting Adolf Deissmann's remark that Paul's was "a life work that as a mere physical performance challenges our admiration." "The most powerful human personality in the history of the Church . . . The influence of Pauline thought has permeated all subsequent theology" is another authoritative comment. James Stewart, one of Paul's ablest modern interpreters, is content to call him history's "greatest saint".

There is, nevertheless, something a little odd in thus measuring, comparing, and classifying one whose towering achievement, many-sided character, and obvious divine inspiration appear to set him apart from ordinary human judgements. To most Christians, Paul is just "the great apostle", his writings are "scripture", and his life work is ascribed directly to his Lord. That is, perhaps, the highest possible compliment to any servant of Christ.

All estimates of a Christian's contribution to God's cause are tentative, and partial; yet in Paul's case the verdict of history is clear: the life that Paul lived was epoch-making in the most literal sense, as one of those rare lives in which time turns a corner and a new age begins. Far beyond his own imagining, or the understanding of his contemporaries, Paul engraved his name deeply on the story of mankind as one of the makers of Europe, and indeed of the whole Western world; for the things he wrote and stood for became the unquestioned assumptions of the whole medieval way of life, upon which modern civilisation in the West was built.

Paul's great truth, learned from Christ but first clearly grasped by him among the apostles, was the universality of the gospel. Paul's great task was to found Churches in all the strategic centres of the Roman Empire. Paul's great legacy was his precious correspondence. Because of what he grasped and taught, the Church passed the frontiers of Palestine and left Judaism behind. Because of what he did, the Church survived the collapse of Rome and lived on through the dark ages. Because of what he experienced and movingly told and courageously argued out, the revelation that had come in Christ was translated, expounded, and established as a world faith.

Thus history's assessment of Paul is that he was a crucial, creative, and compelling personality. Religiously, he spanned within himself the wide advance from the highest pre-Christian faith to mature Christianity. Intellectually, he has quickened and fertilised the thought of two thousand years. Sociologically, he established Christian cells in such number and depth, and initiated the spread of Christianity with such vigour, that the Church became the repository of much of the heritage of the ancient world when Rome fell.

Theologically, it was Paul, more than any other individual, who achieved the transition from Jewish to Gentile categories of thought, preserving meanwhile the essentially Hebraic insights upon which the gospel rests. Spiritually, he has been teacher, guide, pastor, and inspiration, to countless generations of Christ's disciples. "No man is indispensable in the kingdom of God"· to that glib maxim, Paul is the one man in history whom we might consider an exception. No servant of Jesus could desire a higher assessment of his life's work than that!

The verdict of history upon any life gains in perspective but loses in immediacy and vividness: and it is well to set beside the judgement of after ages the assessment of Paul offered by his contemporaries. The life that he lived, they would surely say, was essentially one of personal power. They found that the gospel came to them through him not in word only but in power, and in the Holy Ghost, and in much assurance. The signs of an apostle were wrought before their eyes in patience, and in mighty deeds.

He was mistaken for Mercury, messenger of gods, an impressive tribute to his persuasiveness of speech and to the sense of more than human authority that accompanied his preaching. He came to Corinth in weakness and in fear and with much trembling, yet speaking in demonstration of the Spirit and of power. On board a doomed ship, his "presence" commands attention amid panic. Weak, ill and aged, he remained the centre of a team of vigorous younger men.

He himself knew that virtue went out of him, as his words about instructors and fathers show; he knew that his preaching could kindle life. So men wept at the news that they would see him no longer, because he could kindle drooping faith, awaken slumbering hopes, impart soaring ideals, nourish weak souls, instruct, rebuke, constrain. He lived and travelled, wrote and preached, suffered and resisted, prayed and wrought, the centre of a growing circle, every member of which owed much to his zeal, his faith, his penetrating mind, his indomitable strength, his endless patience.

And as he could comfort, so he could condemn — the profligate Felix trembled before him, Festus and Agrippa acknowledged the spell of his words, the governor of Cyprus was astonished and won: none of them credulous simpletons spell-bound by any wandering demagogue. This is power: and in his burning messages, bracing faith, stark challenges, and winsome encouragement, men felt the power of Christ resting upon him. Few would ask other assessment of our work than that.

With the verdict of history and the testimony of his contemporaries in mind, it is illuminating to turn to Paul's own account of "the life I now live". He speaks much of physical disability, of temptations, of suffering, shipwreck, stripes, imprisonment, and peril. He feels keenly the scoffing, derision, persecution, of the fellow-Jew, and the occasional criticism of the fellow-Christian. He was always aware that the power he wielded was dearly purchased, by nights of agony, days of toil, and hours of fierce temptation fiercely fought.

"I know how to be abased . . . I have learned the secret of enduring want . . . the sufferings of Christ abound in us . . . we were pressed out of measure, above our strength, insomuch that we despaired of life . . . Out of much affliction and anguish of heart I wrote to you with many tears. We are troubled on every side . . . perplexed, persecuted, cast down: always bearing about in the body the dying of the Lord Jesus, always delivered unto death for Jesus' sake, the outward man perishing."

On the subject of his sufferings Paul becomes almost

lyrical, with his labours, stripes, perils of all kinds, weariness watchings, nakedness, care. "We are a spectacle unto angels and to men, buffetted and homeless, reviled and defamed fools, weak, despised, the filth and offscouring of all things unto this day."

To all this must be added infirmity, and inceasing effort, and the constant, unremitting spiritual tension of a soul ever at stretch, the unrelenting conflict against his own temptations. "Not as though I had already attained, either were already perfect . . . I press toward the mark . . . I therefore so run . . . so fight: I keep under my body . . . lest I should be disqualified."

This is Paul's own assessment of the life he lived – a life of hardship borne through Christ's strength, of suffering softened by grace, of burdens carried only by divine enabling, of pressing dangers, hostility, and calumny, only tolerable because God is constantly at hand.

How very differently the same life looks from within, from without, and afterwards! To us, a measureless world-shaping, time-fashioning success; to his contemporaries, a living demonstration of spiritual power and divine energies; but to himself, a strain of toil and suffering, heartache and rejection. He knew nothing at all of the spiritual status-symbols and trappings of success so coveted among ourselves – no blaze of arc-lights, trumpeted statistics, and glossy photographs! He could not estimate his own success: probably he would not try; but he was fully engaged in an endless task in which men are called not to be successful, but faithful.

Explanations

In attempting to pierce the secrets behind this life Paul lived, to uncover its motivation and analyse its dynamic resources, it is impossible to begin anywhere but with his own self-explanation: "I have been crucified with Christ; it is no longer I who live, but Christ who lives in me; and the life I now live in the flesh I live by faith in the Son of God, who loved me and gave himself for me."

Here the psychiatrist psychoanalyses himself! Here the Christian behind the apostle, the thinker, the warrior, the evangelist, the living martyr, offers his testimony and explains his inmost working attitudes. The basis and beginning of everything with me, and the abiding foundation of my life, Paul says, is the apprehending of Christ. This is Paul's testimony to the sufficiency of faith in his own experience. Here, however, by an unusual turn of phrase, Paul's emphasis falls upon the active, dynamic meaning of "faith": not as decision for Christ, the act of commitment to Christian loyalties and standards; nor as trust, resting upon Christ from the burden of sin and the fear of judgement; but rather as a continuous, day-to-day, laying hold of Christ for strength, inspiration, counsel, courage, hope, sanctification and endurance as the Christian meets new situations, confronts new adversities, attempts new tasks, assumes new responsibilities – and ever finding Christ unfailingly sufficient.

As the faith described is essentially dynamic, so its Object is seen in varied lights, now as the Son of God, in all His power and wisdom, when the soul is weak; now as the One "who gave himself for me", when failure and disappointment recall earlier rebellion, and Paul's confidence is shaken; and now as the One "who loved me", in all His tender concern and compassion, when Paul's suffering is greatest. I live, says the apostle, by perpetually laying hold of the inexhaustible Christ.

Such outward-looking faith necessarily involves turning from oneself. Paul must therefore affirm: the character and quality of my life, its prevailing tone and temper, arise from my identification with Christ. "I have been crucified with Christ; it is no longer I who live." In the words "have been" Paul is probably referring to his initial identification with Christ's death expressed in his baptism, but the "have been" carries with it "still am" – for the sharing of Christ's death to self, to sin, and to the world continues throughout the Christian's career. Christian evangelism calls us to take up the cross and follow Christ to our own Calvary; Christian faith declares that we are dead and our life is hid with Christ in God; Christian baptism affirms that we are "buried with Christ by baptism into death"; the Church's Memorial Supper continually underlines our pledged participation in His passion for the world. Christ died for all, so all died: to live no longer for themselves but for Him who for their sake died and by the power of God was raised again.

This is the negative implication of daily apprehending Christ, and it is, for many of us, the crucial difficulty of the ongoing Christian life – thus constantly to turn away from ourselves and our own supposed spiritual resources, to focus all hope and confidence on Christ. But once again the negative implication cannot stand alone: the mainspring and motive of the life I now live, Paul continues, is the indwelling of Christ. "It is no longer I who live, but Christ who lives in me."

In Paul's most characteristic thinking, Christ came in the fulness of time, but He is not far behind us; He ascended up on high, yet He is not far above us; He will come again, but He is not away ahead of us. He is ever the Christ *within us* – our hope of glory. His love is shed abroad within our hearts, His truth still kindles in our minds, His power and grace are yet expressed through receptive souls. He is the Lord always "at hand". "Christ . . . lives in me" – as though Paul would say, "The life you watch, and wonder at, is not mine at all: it is His – refracted, hindered, impaired, no doubt, by my imperfections – but nevertheless essentially His life flowing through me to heal, to comfort, and to save."

So Paul explains his life and ministry, and the explanation does illumine his historic achievement, his contemporaries' impression, his personal endurance. Such achievements do flow only from the constant apprehending of Christ. Without Christ, even Paul could do nothing; failing this daily appropriation of the living Lord, the most gifted Christian worker is but disconnected plant, all set for operation but powerless; busy, eager, tense, but ineffectual. Only as we lay hold of the limitless resources of Christ, in all the dimensions of His Sonship and Saviourhood, do things happen, and our talents and knowledge and training become of any use in the eternal kingdom. His, and His alone, is the word that illumines, the power that heals, the authority that convinces, and the grace that saves.

In the same way, such sustained struggle as Paul waged, such ability to suffer without bitterness, to endure disappointment without despair, is the natural fruit of crucifixion with Christ. To be so identified with Jesus that self and the flesh are already denied to the point of death is to be immune to most of the wounds men can inflict. What, after all, could Romans or Jews, disloyal colleagues, Judaists, or pagan mobs, do to Paul that he had not willingly accepted when he took his place at Calvary beside his Lord? All that the world could harm, all that sin could tempt, he chose to "reckon dead" already: therein lay Paul's freedom, and courage, his endurance, and his perpetual newness of life.

It was this that his contemporaries felt, an outflow of personal power not to be explained by Paul's own personality, and a spirit whose centres of courage, whatever he suffered, were ultimately beyond the reach of human hostility. Christ lived again in this man, and others contacted Christ in him. And he knew this was truth about himself: "I worked harder than any of them," he says, immediately correcting himself with "though it was not I, but the grace of God which is with me." And again, "In Christ Jesus then I have reason to be proud of my work for God. For I will not venture to speak of anything except what Christ has wrought through me." To understand this, to consent to it, and live and work in the constant awareness of it, demands both humility and faith in equal and exceptional degree: but it is to discover divine energies at work, often in surprising ways, and divine things happening, often in unpropitious times.

20 Energies Evoked from Within

GRANTED THAT PAUL possessed intellectual gifts of a very high order, a unique experience, a passionate temperament, and impetuous eloquence; granted, too, his brilliant Jewish background and providential Roman citizenship; granted, even his intense and selfless consecration to the cause of Christ we still have not explained his glorious achievement. Talent character, and circumstances fit the tool for the task, but the moral and spiritual dynamic that drives the tool effectively lies elsewhere – a truth which we, in our zeal for "efficiency" sometimes overlook.

No study of Paul's portrait would possess much relevance for our time if it did not attempt to discover the source of his astonishing power, and to analyse, as well as can be the forces that moved that dynamic personality so mightily so effectively, and so long. If Paul cannot tell us, then we shall never know where may be found those creative and redemptive energies which even yet may revitalise the twentieth century, regenerate humanity, and save our world from moral and physical destruction.

Directing Forces

The arrow's feathers add nothing to its velocity, yet they contribute greatly to its striking power, by keeping the flight true to its target and so avoiding the dissipation of initial impetus. Paul's strength was conserved, and his energies controlled, by three such directional forces – a "call", a vision, and what we would doubtless call today a "phobia"; and, significantly, each enshrines a point of spiritual tension.

Paul was convinced that God intended him to be a minister. Speaking to Agrippa, and again when writing to Galatia, he relates this conviction to his conversion experience: "I have appeared to you for this purpose, to appoint you to serve . . . God was pleased to reveal his Son to me in order that I might preach him . . ." This may owe something to the telescoping of later reflection – though it is certain that, in Paul's mind, his encounter with the risen Lord constituted his claim to apostleship.

In the Galatian passage, Paul traces this call to divine ervice back to, and before, his birth: God, he says, "had et me apart before I was born." God's gift to him of life tself had this original intention. The word "call", however, s hardly strong enough to convey what Paul felt, for it nakes something depend upon Paul's "answer". Paul would acknowledge this, and twice he says "I became" a minister; out his usual expression is that God "appointed" the ministry n the Church, he was "appointed" a preacher, "was made" a minister.

Born to it, converted to it, appointed to it: so Paul saw his life-work against the background of the over-ruling will of God. Like the Eleven, he could look back to a commission only to be expressed in words like – "You have not chosen me, but I have chosen you and ordained you . . ." It was all of God.

But it is revealing that Paul's assertions of his divine commission are strongest where comparison with others is involved. To the Galatians he disclaims all need to consult "those who were of repute . . . pillars"; and of the Corinthians he enquires "Are they apostles . . . are they ministers of Christ . . . so am I", commenting sharply upon those who "measure themselves by one another and compare themselves with one another", and need "letters of recommendation".

It would be foolish to argue that this defensive tone betrayed a mind unsure of its own apostolic status. But Paul was certainly troubled about being "one untimely born", and so carrying apostolic responsibilities and authority without claim to having been, like Peter, John and the rest, a companion of Jesus. Others knew Christ "from a human point of view" – but this he brushes aside, a little too quickly. Others met the risen Lord, but he demanded – "Am I not an apostle? Have I not seen Jesus our Lord?" His answer to certain disparaging comparisons is, that God has called, and taught, and chosen, and commissioned him. What in some men might have bred destructive self-doubt and uncertainty, in Paul fed the strong conviction that he would surely not be where he was but for God.

Some earnest men, truly dedicated to Christ's service, have reached the point where the sense of personal commission fails, cancelled out by disappointment, by frustration, by opposition, perplexity, mistakes, perhaps by foolish neglect of the means of grace which hearts ministering to others need more than all. In the confusion and heartache of such an experience, it is hard to understand what constitutes a special vocation to Christian service – whether talent, aptitude, earnest desire, prayerful dedication free from self-seeking, the approval of experienced and impartial counsellors, or "signs following"?

Paul does not reduce the call to wholly subjective impulse, or inward impression concerning the will of God. Before Timothy was appointed, he was well-reported of by the brethren at Lystra and Derbe, and in the Pastoral letters much emphasis is laid upon proved character and aptitude in those chosen for leadership. Paul is prepared, too, to appeal for confirmation of his own authority to the "signs of an apostle" wrought among the Corinthians; and when he calls the Corinthians his "letters of recommendation", he both witnesses to such a custom among the Churches and comments that the living convert is better than the most flattering testimonial!

Yet neither will Paul allow the criticism of others, or disappointment with results, or the knowledge of his own temptations, to destroy his certainty that God had made him a minister. Knowing the sincerity of his own heart, he held to that conviction with humility but also with tenacious courage. In the last resort, a man's sense of "call" is inexplicable, entirely personal, in nature "existential", and not to be rationalised or proved. It is for him a matter of living encounter with God; of a command laid upon his soul which he must obey – or disobey. In dark, frustrating days, it becomes an issue of blind faith in God's faithfulness.

Like all God's greater servants, Paul knew both the deep strength, and the painful tensions, in which that call involved him. But it held him to his task, multiplied his power, nerved his costly endurance, by unifying all the energies of his nature around a dominating – but not self-chosen – purpose.

That purpose, however, had unique scope. In the terms of the record, it was to carry Christ's name before the Gentiles, and kings, and the sons of Israel; to be sent far away to the Gentiles; to preach Christ among the Gentiles. This universalist vision prompted his active pioneering of new countries and strategic centres, as history's most restless evangelist, as clearly as it informed his theological contention for a gospel addressed to the faith of all men. Paul knew that God had called him, and knew what for: to build the world kingdom of his Lord. Those twin convictions directed all his life.

Sensitive to much of the appeal made by Stoicism, Paul felt the influence of the new humanitarianism beginning to permeate society, with the idea of a brotherhood "of one blood", which should include most races and all classes — even slaves. Stoic pantheism nourished such thoughts — "For we are indeed his offspring" — and the notion of a world-soul binding all creation together made for world-horizons in human relationships. So, too, did the idea of a universal law written by nature upon human hearts. It was an easy step to talking about a world unity of humanity, novel though such a notion was in those days. To such hopes, and gropings, Paul could speak persuasively of the world Church of Jesus, a fellowship embracing in one faith Jew, Greek, Barbarian, male and female, bound and free; and of the universal Christ, in whom all things in heaven and on earth would be reconciled to unity.

Awareness of this philosophic universalism only deepened in Paul's mind the influence of that other, political, universalism which derived from his appreciation of Rome's greatness and purpose. His friendly attitude to Roman officials, his choice of itineraries and centres, his teaching upon citizenship, and his final appeal to Caesar's justice, all express this understanding of the strength and unity of Rome's vision, and when he declared his own purpose to range farther west to Spain, it is evident he was dreaming of a world Empire of Jesus commensurate with that of Caesar. Neither Stoicism nor Roman imperialism taught Paul a world-gospel; Jesus did that. But Paul's intellectual sympathy with the trends of thought of his time help to explain why he grasped so clearly and so soon the meaning of Jesus, and defended so vigorously the vision of the world-wide Church.

Yet Paul was a Jew. He inherited, and was trained to defend, an outlook precisely opposite to Christian, Stoic and Roman universalism. That the change in his thought was neither rapid nor easy is obvious from the tangles Paul gets into when he discusses the special and unchanged election of the Jew to privilege and priority in the purpose of God, and tries to combine with it the truth that Jews have no special advantages in the gospel, for all are one in Christ Jesus. There are tangles, indeed, in exposition: but no doubt where Paul's heart lies. Utterly convinced that the universalist vision is no mirage but God's truth, he throws all the more energy into fulfilling it because he must justify it, both to his countrymen and to himself. His personal inner conflict only lends warmth to his arguments and zeal to his pioneering. To the world kingdom of Christ all his strength was unsparingly dedicated.

The "phobia", or perhaps more accurately the deep-seated aversion, which also powerfully shaped Paul's thought and attitudes, was his fear of pride, or boasting. It may be that Paul had pondered with especial care Christ's strictures upon Pharisaic self-righteousness; it may be that Paul suffered such revulsion at finding himself disastrously wrong in persecuting the Church that he ever after suspected every hint of pride; it could be that he had been sickened by the prevailing vice of Judaism, and knew that Gentile dislike of Jews was justified on this point; possibly, as his letter to Philippi suggests, Paul was especially attracted and impressed by the Servant-character of Jesus: one of these circumstances, or all together, certainly made the once proud Pharisee the very humblest of Christians. This is where the Christian shoe pinched the Jewish foot, and made Paul limp thereafter.

He protests so often: where is boasting, then, – it is excluded; not of works, lest any should boast; no flesh should glory in His presence; he that glorieth, let him glory in the Lord; why dost thou glory as if thou hadst not received all that you possess; though I preach, I have nothing to glory of – it is not expedient for me to glory; though I desire to glory, I shall be a fool; I might also have confidence in the flesh – yet these things I counted loss for Christ; God forbid that I should glory, save in the cross of the Lord Jesus. The root-word "boasting",

'glorying", occurs no less than *fifty-four* times — clear
ymptom of Paul's constant preoccupation with this danger.
This is not all: the temptation is, so to speak, turned inside
ut, and he developes an almost masochist interest in self-
umiliation, self-abnegation, self-crucifixion. He glories —
hat word again! — in infirmities, necessities, tribulation,
'weakness", because then he is "strong". This is more than
rritating paradox: it is Paul's personal reply to Judaism on
he ultimate peril of all religion — self-righteousness. One
annot truly understand Paul until full account is taken of
his deliberate inversion of Pharisaic pride, concentrating
ll energies upon his work and not himself, and making him
he unhindering vehicle of the power Christ laid upon him.

Such are Paul's directing forces, each involved in tension.
Paul is, in himself, a threefold paradox — "unaccredited"
postle, universalist Jew, and humble Pharisee! But Paul had
earned to capitalise his tensions. Inward conflicts that
night destroy another only lent greater force to the apostle's
ersonality: much of his astonishing strength is the multiple
f inward mental and emotional stresses that have not been
ancelled out, or resolved into placid unity — Paul's remained
turbulent, effervescent, far-from-placid temperament — but
ave been deliberately made to serve the overmastering pur-
ose of his life.

Such harnessing of tensions is at least as effective, as
ocially useful, as spiritually fruitful, as any other way of
lealing with inward disharmonies. Men of Paul's calibre
emind us that equilibrium and balance, an "adjusted" out-
ook and emotional poise, are not the only ends in life. Our
working strength is too often only the residue left when one
ide of us has fought and conquered the other: but ordinary
ouls can ill afford to waste any of the intellectual, moral,
motional or religious "drives" available to them — and to
pend strength balancing oneself upon a stationary position
is entirely stultifying. Paul chose the much more painful way
f continuing to see many sides of every question, to feel
many contrary impulses and sympathies, to hold the many-
ided truth refusing facile simplifications; to go on being
Jew, Roman and Christian, called out of due time, universalist sure of divine election, proud of some things while

striving to be humble in all – and to let the resulting strains and tensions kindle the greater energies and amplify his strength.

Driving Forces

If the feathers that held the arrow of Paul's life true to its mark were his call, his vision, and his dread of self-glorying, the bow-string which imparted its original impetus was a threefold cord of fear, love and responsibility.

Fear is no longer a respectable religious motive-force: but how else can one describe the emotion that penned "We must all appear before the judgement seat of Christ, so that each one may receive good or evil, according to what he has done in the body. Therefore, knowing the fear of the Lord, we persuade men . . ."? Paul is, of all New Testament writers, the most haunted by thoughts of final judgement. As he sees the wrath of God revealed against all ungodliness, in the moral decay of society, so is he equally sure – as he declared at Athens – that God "has fixed a day in which he will judge the world in righteousness by a man whom he has appointed . . ."

He argues with the Romans: "We know that the judgement of God rightly falls on those who do such things . . . But by your hard and impenitent heart you are storing up wrath for yourself on the day of wrath when God's righteous judgement will be revealed. For he will render to every man according to his works: to those who by patience in well-doing seek for glory and honour and immortality, he will give eternal life; but for those who are factious and do not obey the truth, but obey wickedness, there will be wrath and fury."

This strong conception of divine judgement as universal, and as essentially moral, is wholly in accord with the judgement-parables of Jesus; and it is the background of Paul's solemn warnings to his fellow-workers: "We shall all stand before the judgement seat of God . . . each of us shall give account of himself to God." True, "there is . . . now no condemnation for those who are in Christ Jesus": but "each man's work will become manifest; for the Day will disclose it, because it will be revealed with fire, and the fire will test what sort of work each one has done. If the work which any man has built . . . survives, he will receive a reward. If any man's work is burned up, he will suffer loss, though he himself will be saved."

"Who are you," he asks, as though surprised at the readers' temerity, "to pass judgement on the servant of another? It is before his own master that he stands or falls." And once again, "It is the Lord who judges me. Therefore do not pronounce judgement before the time, before the Lord comes, who will bring to light the things now hidden in darkness and will disclose the purposes of the heart. Then every man will receive his commendation from God." This is not rhetoric: it unveils one of the deep inner forces of Paul's life – the constant fear "lest after preaching to others I myself should be disqualified".

We are inescapably reminded of Christ's words about the reckoning of the returning Lord with His servants, in saying after saying. But behind this memory, in Paul's mind, lay also the long Jewish hinterland of thought about God as the Lawgiver and Judge and the universe as essentially moral. "Do not be deceived; God is not mocked, for whatever a man sows, that he will also reap" is counsel as native to Judaism as to Christianity – and indeed to all serious thought about the nature of the moral life. Must moderns always wince at this idea? Man is either a moral idiot, set within a universe morally chaotic, or he is a responsible being set within an *order* where consequences are linked logically and morally with causes; and where moral education, worth, and progress, praise and blame, are therefore possible. Modern Christianity needs to relearn that there is neither reason nor profit in denying the reality of judgement: it would put iron into our souls, and new urgency into our work, to share Paul's godly fear of "the terror of the Lord".

Immediately upon his mention of fear, however, Paul names second among his driving forces the love of Christ – a motive as compulsive and consuming in his public endeavour and endurance as it was in his more private consecration. Answering the charge of being "beside ourselves", he says "the love of Christ *controls* us", using the forceful word which elsewhere describes the multitude hemming in Jesus on every side, the Roman armies investing Jerusalem, and Christ being hampered and constrained in spirit by His approaching passion. Paul seems to imply: "this is the madness that is upon us; that is the 'possession' that explains our eccentric behaviour: the love of Christ has seized us, forcibly constrains us, holds us prisoners to His will."

Such love informed and influenced Paul's thinking: "we are convinced that one has died for all; therefore all have died". It found expression also in the moral redirection of life's energies: "he died for all, that those who live might live no longer for themselves but for him . . ." Yet it was essentially emotional, moving the heart with passionate affection and an ardent delight in Christ. Deeply emotional language to describe the relation of Christians to their Lord is admittedly out of fashion. Until we have rescued the language of love from Freud and the sexicologists we shall never be able again to use it with ease in religious contexts – though Bernard of Clairvaux, St. Francis of Assisi, Judson, or Rutherfurd, would find our hesitation very strange.

Nevertheless, much devotional poetry borrows freely from sexual imagery, and the psychological reason is not far to seek: Paul himself suggests it. His assertions of his right to marry, his argument about the value of marriage as the best moral antidote to concupiscence, his frequent use of metaphors of marriage and parenthood, and his strong references to keeping his body in subjection, all gain significance in the light of modern psychoanalysis, and tend to confirm the hints in Romans 7 that all was not always well with Paul's emotional life.

When therefore he argues that the unmarried are anxious about the affairs of the Lord, and how to please Him, whereas the married are anxious to please each other, and advises that the Corinthians remain unmarried and give their undivided devotion to the Lord, we wonder how far he is really arguing with himself! The counsel is short-sighted, one-sided, and a little inhuman; it must not be forgotten that human love, too, is a divine gift; or that Paul himself elsewhere urges Christians to witness for their Lord by the quality of their home-life. How far the apparent lack of wife and family circle lent fervour to Paul's Christian devotion, we might hesitate to say, but in any case his comparison of human with sacred love gives strong indication of the emotional depth of Paul's love for Christ. Whatever the truth about Paul's own temptations, it is certain that his reaction was not mere repression but the redirection of every emotional drive of his strong nature into his love for his Lord.

In the same context with fear and love for Christ, Paul makes much of his ambassadorship for the gospel, declaring that high responsibility to be twofold: towards those to whom the ambassador is sent, charged to persuade, to convince and win by all legitimate arts of diplomacy and advocacy — "We beseech you"; and towards his sovereign, whose policy and will he serves — "We beseech you on behalf of Christ."

This sense of being entrusted by high Authority with a vital responsibility is expressed in many ways. Paul feels a personal concern for unbelieving Israel, although their unbelief is their own fault: "I am speaking the truth . . . I am not lying . . . I have great sorrow and unceasing anguish in my heart. For I could wish that I myself were accursed and cut off from Christ for the sake of my brethren, my kinsmen by race." He carries upon his heart the weak and shallow brother endangered by the free conduct of stronger Christians: for him, sinning against one's brethren and wounding their weak conscience is sinning against Christ; "if food is a cause of my brother's falling, I will never eat meat, lest I cause my brother to fall."

Paul had the same sense of responsibility about preaching: "Necessity is laid upon me . . . Woe to me if I do not preach the gospel." And he had, to an infinite degree, the pastor's heart: "Apart from all other things there is the daily pressure upon me of my anxiety for all the churches. Who is weak, and I am not weak? Who is made to fall, and I am not indignant?" The same costly identification with others sharpens the expostulations with the Galatians, and intensifies the "anguish and many tears" of the Corinthian correspondence.

Responsibility may seem too cold a word for so compelling a motive-force in Paul's career: care, concern, good will, sympathy, and love are all implied. But it was something deeper and more lasting, and more costly, than the impulsive response of a sensitive heart to particular cases of need: it was a sustained moral effort of accepted accountability to Christ for kinsmen, converts, brethren and Churches, a voluntary spiritual obligation which drove Paul to endless labour, unfailing patience, and great sacrifice.

So deeply, so intimately, had Paul entered into the spirit of Jesus, and into the meaning of vicarious redemption. This is the responsibility of the shepherd who must leave the ninety and nine and go after the lost hundredth until he find it; of the physician whose help is vital to them that are sick; of the Saviour who comes to seek and to save them that are lost; of the Servant who "took our infirmities . . . carried our sorrows . . . bore our sins". As Christ voluntarily accepted our responsibilities, so Paul accepted responsibility for all in need – as a necessary evangelical compulsion upon his own spirit. He was constantly impelled by the clear realisation that in such steadfast, voluntary concern by One for many lay the sole means of his own salvation, and the very spirit of the cross in which he gloried.

Fear of Christ's displeasure, love for Christ Himself, and vicarious responsibility for others in Christ's name, form a triplet of Christian motive forces that explain a great soul and a tremendous achievement. Sometimes one driving compulsion, sometimes another, might answer the need of the moment, might dispel disappointment, nerve to further peril, or constrain to new attempting. Together, they can still keep a man striving with unflagging energies at the towering task until his strength and life are spent and life's work is done.

Defensive Forces

Firm directing convictions, and strong compulsive motives, however, are not wholly sufficient: the servant of God is not immune from the dangers to faith, integrity, and humility, that beset all Christians, but especially those in the public eye. It is easy to grow secretly cynical, or merely professional; to lose the sense of being personally involved in the things taught to others, in the duties urged upon others, in the troubles others bring for help and healing. Few escape entirely the temptations to self-righteousness, to vanity, to self-seeking and the love of praise. The more earnest the worker, the more prone to despondency – the dangerous, undermining discouragement that can miss God's opportunity through unreadiness, or refuse God's challenges for want of faith in His presence and power.

So Paul names for us the secrets of unfainting service and unwearying vigilance for one's own soul, among them two which may be said to be "energies evoked from within" – the unfading memory of God's great mercy, and the steadfast hope of eternal success.

Among Paul's reflections upon his conversion, one conviction stood out, and remained through all the pressures and perils of his varied life, that he had experienced in himself a true miracle of sovereign, inexplicable mercy. His many later references to earlier days reveal an unpardoning memory: it is not too much to say that Paul spent himself prodigally in the effort to forgive himself. Such are the words which no-one would have written but himself: "I formerly blasphemed and persecuted and insulted him: but I received mercy . . . and the grace of our Lord overflowed for me . . . I am the foremost of sinners; but I received mercy for this reason, that in me, as the foremost, Jesus Christ might display his perfect patience for an example . . ."

"I persecuted the church of God violently and tried to destroy it", he tells the Galatians; to the Philippians, with wry irony, he offers as evidence of his pre-Christian zeal for religion the confession that he was "a persecutor of the church". "I am unfit to be called an apostle," he admits even to the Corinthians, "because I persecuted the church of God"; and addressing the crowd in the Temple courtyard at Jerusalem, he again recalls his persecuting career, emphasising how thoroughly he had pursued the Church. Before Agrippa, he details the methods of his campaign against the Christians, and the authority he exercised, but he allows himself no loophole of excuse by stressing that he acted "in raging fury" and "myself convinced that I ought to do many things in opposing the name of Jesus of Nazareth."

Such self-analysing memories reveal the degree of self-reproach which Paul carried locked within his heart. We have his own testimony that on at least one occasion (doubtless one of many) the painful memory intruded even into his prayers: "I said, Lord, they themselves know that in every synagogue I imprisoned and beat those who believed in thee, and when the blood of thy witness Stephen was shed I also was standing by and approving." And it lingered long in his thoughts that the first words he had ever heard from the lips of the risen Lord were, "Saul, Saul, why persecutest thou me?"

Here, again, something that might have destroyed another man, precluding all spiritual endeavour, clouding all faith, creating all kinds of spiritual sickness — obsessive introspection, maladjustment, self-depreciation, possibly by inversion even a persecution complex — in Paul became a constant spur to greater effort, a persistent striving to overtake the past and undo the things he could only recall with pain. What might have inhibited, in fact inspired; and the remembered guilt became transmuted into moral drive.

This is the gospel's unrivalled remedy for wrong. Where psychiatry might have said "bring the guilt into daylight and learn to live with it"; where moralism would have said "repent and forget"; where even "cheap grace" evangelicalism might have said "confess, and it is as though it had never been", Paul's deeper gospel says "do not forget, or excuse, or pretend it never happened, or live within the unrelieved shadow of its memory: rest on the divine mercy for the past and sublimate memory into moral incentive." Much of the explanation of Paul's stupendous career lies in the words, "As we have received mercy, we faint not." It is the glory of redeeming grace that, given penitence and faith, it transforms evil into good, and mercy received becomes itself an unfailing resource for unfainting zeal.

The second defensive secret of unfainting service and unwearying vigilance is named in the same passage: "This slight momentary affliction is preparing for us an eternal weight of glory beyond all comparison, because we look not to the things that are seen but to the things that are unseen; for the things that are seen are transient, but the things that are unseen are eternal."

In such courageous words is revealed a prevailing attitude of mind which yields endless spiritual resource. By such insights, and on such far-seeing principles, he judged the progress of the kingdom and the success or failure of his own work. His certainty of immortality, and of the "Day of

Christ" yet to come, gave perspective and understanding to all his thinking about the gospel and the world. He reckons upon "things eternal" in every common day, and can himself stand fast, immovable, always abounding in the work of the Lord, because he knows that his labour is not in vain in Christ.

Something is here of the incentive of reward. A crown is laid up for him, of life completed, of righteousness fulfilled, of glory won. Even more attractive is the hope of departing to be with Christ "for that is far better". And such hope of reward has ample foundation in the promises of Jesus. But in the words cited there is more perhaps of the undergirding insight into all historical processes and human situations which was native to Hebrew faith and passed thence into Christian belief. "The world passes away", and all its works, lusts, and pride. That is no cause for dismay, nor of surprise, to Hebrew-Christian eyes. Things seen are creaturely, and therefore transient: once they were not, and again they shall not be — but God abides.

He remaineth. His throne is for ever and ever, and His will is steadfast, His love enduring, His purpose unchanging, His patience exhaustless. So beneath the surface of the things seen, are the forces of truth and right, and of redemption, that only "spiritual" eyes discern and only faithful hearts can understand. Paul's deep faith echoes the defiant, disdainful confidence of the Psalmist: "The nations rage, the kingdoms totter; he utters his voice — the earth melts!"

For a heart so tireless, forceful, impatient for good, restlessly energetic, this confidence is very far from fatalism or complacency. But it did yield an imperturbable mind, a serene spirit, which could endure in face of great adversity and disappointment, holding its course by the same stars which fought against Sisera, and riding the currents that, despite all the surface flow of a threatening sea, bear steadily onwards to the kingdom of God.

There is little satisfaction in striving to analyse a great heart. Motives, energies, spiritual resources are elusive quantities in all of us — how much more so in a soul as tremendous and as complicated as Paul's! Yet even to see so much of what he has chosen to reveal is to realise again how shallow our own lives are, and the forces that could yet be released within our own hearts if we lived, as Paul did, truly "in Christ".

21 Power Conferred from Above

ARE WE THEN TO resolve the colossal impact of this extraordinary career into a pattern of psychological motivations, into native energies evoked by a unique series of experiences? Do the biographical details, the paradoxical tensions and personal reactions, account for everything – given the forceful temperament, the exceptional talent, and historical circumstances shaped to offer the resultant personality an adequate opportunity?

How vigorously, even violently, Paul would say No! His "not I, but Christ" is the brief, blunt, effective answer to all attempts to "explain" Paul on merely humanistic and psychological terms. Reputedly "little of stature", he yet defies measurement unless an unambiguous "vertical dimension" be allowed for, an "enduement from on high", to borrow his companion's phrase. The evocation, and harnessing, of such inherent spiritual powers was itself something of a miracle, and demands further explanation. As his own experience of salvation was, in Paul's eyes, all of grace, so any achievement to be ascribed to his life-work was, equally to his eyes, all of God. To deny this would be to deny his gospel of "supernatural" salvation, and to challenge the divine origin and authority of his apostleship.

Confidence in the constant co-operation of divine forces becomes a crucial matter for every conscientious servant of God when the first excitements of Christian work have passed and consecration must be translated into long, sustained, consistent labour, in season and out of season, with evident fruitfulness or without. Paul counted upon such assistance, not only in the daily renewal of his own inward life at its everlasting fountains, but also in the effective wielding of what may pardonably be called his "operating" forces – the means upon which he relied to accomplish the work of the gospel.

Inward Renewal

Commenting upon the inherent spiritual forcefulness of one of the greatest missionary statesmen of our time, John Raleigh Mott, Temple Gairdner said, "Such consistent power is vested in no man save him in whom it daily accumulates by habitual communion with the one Source." That is a sentence to which it is easy to imagine Paul's saying a fervent "Amen". Among his personal centralities, prominence was given to his "mystical" conception of life "in Christ" —a union with the living Lord which provided the very atmosphere Paul breathed and the sustenance by which his soul was nourished. Recalling this, we are not surprised that he should name, among the forces that kept him from "fainting" – from the spiritual exhaustion that in ardent and prodigal hearts too often spells breakdown – a continual inward refreshment that matched the demands of his work.

"So we do not lose heart. Though our outer nature is wasting away, our inner nature is being renewed every day." What he means by the "outer nature wasting away" is perfectly clear: "We are afflicted on every side . . . perplexed . . . persecuted . . . struck down . . . always carrying in the body the death of Jesus . . . always being given up to death for Jesus' sake. Death is at work in us . . ." These are not metaphors for gloomy moods, but daily experiences: they epitomise Paul's life of endurance and conflict; and its effect upon his body and upon his natural energies is quite realistically expressed – "our outer nature is wasting away".

What he means therefore by the "inner nature being renewed every day" is likewise a matter of experience and realism. It is certainly not a metaphor for cheering himself up! Nor does he mean, merely, that he knows the healing power of inward quietness and retreat, or that he lives by praying. It is not prayer, but the answers to prayer, that provide his resource; an objective, divine assistance received from the living Christ. "The life also of Jesus [is] manifested in our bodies", "the life of Jesus [is] manifested in our mortal flesh." This is the miracle of spiritual refreshment – not the reviving of our energies only, but the reinforcement of ours with His.

The result is not immunity from suffering or distress, but it is immunity from breakdown and failure: "We are afflicted, but not crushed; perplexed, but not driven to despair; persecuted but not forsaken; struck down but not destroyed." And whatever is happening to us, Paul continues, "life is at work in you."

Paul refers in two other passages to this "inward nature" or "inner man". In the letter to the Romans the allusion is mainly to the "mind" as contrasted with the emotional nature and its appetites. Here Paul declares that he delights in the law of God in his "inmost self", and doubtless we are justified in inferring that such "delight in the law of the Lord" was to him (as to the Psalmist, especially dear to all Rabbinic hearts), a sending down of the roots of the soul "like a tree planted by streams of water, that yields its fruit in its season, and its leaf does not wither. In all that he does he prospers." That Paul's mind was "renewed day by day" by "every word that proceeds from the mouth of God" needs no proof.

In the letter to the Ephesians, too, Paul's reference to the "inward nature" is likewise concerned with accessions of strength, and here the allusion is to the whole inward life of the soul, including both the "heart" in which Christ dwells, and the mind which "comprehends" with all saints the breadth, length, height and depth of the love of God. Paul prays that the Ephesian Christians may be "strengthened with might through God's Spirit in the inner man" and suggests as the measure of strength available "the riches of his glory." The letter is full of the thought of God's power, especially as demonstrated in the resurrection and ascension of Jesus and the divine conquest of all evil forces in the universe; and this is the might by which the Christian may be inwardly renewed as Christ dwells within him by faith.

It is perhaps not easy to imagine Paul engaged with eager diligence in daily poring over the word of God at his devotions, or in daily *exercising* his faith in Christ, stretching its capacity, flexing its muscles, in some new direction, or in daily opening his soul by penitence, confession, submission, adoration, to the divine indwelling of the mighty Christ. But it is certain he did so, never attempting to live upon his own inward resources only. "He lived by the laying hold of Christ" — and found himself renewed.

And so, day by day, the consistent power "accumulated".

The Living Word

Turning from the power conferred upon the worker to the forces operative within the work, there is little doubt that

Paul would ascribe much of the effectiveness of his ministry to inherent, dynamic energies within the word he preached. To the prominent place Paul gave to preaching in the divine process of salvation, and the confidence he possessed in the power of his gospel, even when confronting Rome, and the existential note demanding immediate decision which was part of his message, must now be added Paul's conviction that the actual word spoken, the truth uttered by his lips, was *itself* a living energy of God. The gospel constituted in itself an effectual, operative utterance of God, brought to bear, by preaching, upon the minds and the hearts of those who heard.

We should not be unfamiliar with the idea of a "living word", for the opening chapter of the Bible shows the dynamic utterance of God the Creator in majestic action. God said – and it was so. So also in the New Testament: "By faith we understand that the world was created by the word of God"; and again, "by the word of God heavens existed long ago, and an earth . . ."

"So shall my word be that goes forth from my mouth" says God through the prophet: "it shall not return to me empty, but it shall accomplish that which I purpose, and prosper in the thing for which I sent it." Even the Law declares: "Man does not live by bread alone, but . . . by everything that proceeds out of the mouth of the Lord"; and the Psalmist replies, "He sent forth his word and healed them." With one voice the Hebrew thinkers testify that the spoken word of the living God is a vehicle of divine life and power, bearing at once the authority and the effectual energy to accomplish the divine intent. That assumption lends additional sting to the repeated scorn about *"dumb* idols".

"Only say the word and my servant will be healed" said one accustomed to words of command, to a Master in whom he perceived similar executive power of speech. "The word", reiterates Luke concerning the gospel, "*grew* and was multiplied . . . *grew* and prevailed"; and later Peter and James agree that it is by the living word that souls are reborn and nourished, by an *engrafted* or *implanted* word (the metaphors are always drawn from living things), which is *seed,* inducing new birth as a vitalising agent within the soul. The writer to the Hebrews summarises truth important to Christians and to Jews alike in asserting that "the word of God is living and active, sharper than any two-edged sword, piercing to the division of soul and spirit . . . discerning the thoughts and intentions of the heart."

Paul, naturally, shared this conception to the full. The word "is not bound" but a free and moving power; even human words are more than breath and sound, they are conduct, action – "Whatsoever you do, in word or deed . . ." – how much more is the spoken word of God an act of God. Life came to men who "obeyed from the heart" the form of teaching delivered by Christ's witnesses, that "word of the truth of the gospel" which came to the Colossians as indeed to the whole world, "bearing fruit and growing . . ." The seal of the Spirit, the guarantee of a redeemed inheritance, came to the Ephesians through the hearing of "the word of truth". Even more clearly is this expressed in the letter to Thessalonica: "We also thank God constantly for this, that when you received the word of God which you heard from us, you accepted it not as the word of men but as what it really is, *the word of God which is at work* in you believers."

The fundamental truth appears to be that God is, so to speak, committed by His word to take effective action, and present in His word to accomplish what He pleases. Where the word of God is being spoken, there God Himself is already working. In receiving the word by faith's assent and trust, the believer is taking into his soul a seed or principle of new life, in which light, morality, joy and power are implanted. He is, by so hearing, being born again, "begotten", created anew, by the life-bearing, quickening word which is the gospel.

If, however, the word be not believed, Paul is no less certain that it works, still, with divine authority and power. But now in judgement. Paul would echo the warning of Jesus: "Take heed how ye hear!" For each pronouncement of the gospel message was crucial in the fullest sense of an existential crisis for the hearer. If, as at Antioch in Pisidia, and later at Corinth, and later still at Rome, the preaching was by some rejected, then Paul at once pronounced judgement and turned to others.

This is the Pauline equivalent of John's "he who does not believe is condemned already . . . he who does not obey shall not see life, the wrath of God abideth on him; he who hears my word and believes . . . has eternal life . . . has passed from death to life." For Paul firmly believed that whenever he preached, divine, eternal things happened, for good or ill. He, preaching the gospel, actually brought the savour of life to some, the smell of death to others: they lived, or they perished, by their response.

Consistently with this profound confidence in the inherent power within the preached word, Paul eschewed the aids of human wisdom and studied eloquence, that the faith of his converts might rest, not in enticing words but in the power of God. When he deliberately sets his message – "Jesus Christ, and him crucified" in sharp contrast with the wisdom of this world, the "cleverness of the clever", the "debater of the age", the test which he applies to decide which is worthwhile is just this test of inherent power: "the word of the cross is folly to those who are perishing, but to us who are being saved it is the power of God."

Such was the first of Paul's "operating" forces: the spiritual dynamic native to and inherent within the message itself, proclaimed with sincerity, in the authority of the divine call, with a passion for men and in a spirit of love, and focussed in Christ risen, the Lord and Judge. Convinced thus of the effectual power of the word he preached, he firmly believed that in the last resort men "cannot do anything against the truth, but only for the truth."

The Awakened Conscience

The second operating force upon which Paul relied lies within the human soul. In the exquisite parable of "The Seed Growing Secretly", Jesus says "the earth produces of itself." Within the context of the parable, that unexpected phrase suggests that the soil of human nature possesses within itself forces that co-operate with the scattered seed and enable it to "sprout and grow . . . first the blade, then the ear, then the full grain in the ear."

Even more clearly, Jesus appeals to the witness to truth within the soul in a saying of crucial importance for the understanding of His own method. "When you see a cloud rising in the west, you say at once, 'A shower is coming'; and so it happens. And when you see the south wind blowing, you say, 'There will be scorching heat'; and it happens. You hypocrites! You know how to interpret the appearance of earth and sky; but why do you not know how to interpret the present time? And why do you not judge for yourselves what is right?"

This appeal to the inner moral sense of ordinary folk is entirely characteristic of Jesus. It explains His refusal to argue; it prompts His constant questions, throwing the onus of admission upon the hearer; it lends to some of the parables and discourses almost the nature of conversation — "Which of you has a friend . . . What father among you . . . What do you think? If a man has a hundred sheep . . . What do you think? A man had two sons . . . Those eighteen upon whom the tower in Siloam fell . . . Do you think they were worse offenders than all the others . . . ? How is it that you fail to perceive . . ."

This is much more than a grace of speech: it is an appeal directly to the conscience of the hearer in all circumstances and upon all topics, as to an ally of the truth already entrenched within the hearer's soul. And Paul learned well this method of the Master, to make conscience, and not mind alone, or feeling alone, the target for the message.

"By the open statement of the truth we would commend ourselves to every man's conscience in the sight of God." A double faith informs that statement of evangelistic policy: faith in the candid exposition of the message, and faith in the universal conscience. There must be no attempt to dress up the truth in the meretricious garments of rhetoric, special pleading, or false promises: "We have renounced disgraceful and underhanded ways; we refuse to practise cunning or to tamper with God's word." Truth must be made plain, and even palatable. The obstacles in men's minds need to be faithfully removed, sometimes by better information, sometimes by argument and persuasiveness. Moreover truth must be aptly and fittingly spoken, so as to move the heart and kindle appreciation. The appeal to conscience is no cloak for intellectually slipshod presentation, clumsy or blundering exposition, or a dogmatic, aggressive contempt for others' judgement of the message.

Yet, when all care and skill are given to the proclamation of the eternal truth in terms at once relevant, intelligible, and persuasive, it remains important that the preacher does not allow the intellectualist to deflect him from his chosen ground. The evangelist's line of attack is ever by stating the truth with all possible simplicity and power, and demanding not so much agreement with an argument as decision in the presence of Christ the Lord, before God the Judge. Mind is the channel, emotion the agent, the will is the court of appeal, but conscience is unquestionably, for Paul as for Jesus, the target at which the truth is aimed. Even of unbelievers Paul could confidently write "Their conscience bears witness . . ." He knew the added power to be obtained by thus addressing himself to truth's sounding board within the soul.

Yet *preaching* the gospel, even to conscience, is only one half of the evangelical situation. He who appeals to conscience had best be conscientious! "Our boast is this," the apostle tells the Corinthians, "the testimony of our conscience that we have behaved in the world, and still more toward you, with holiness and godly sincerity, not by earthly wisdom but by the grace of God . . ." Again, "we are not, like so many, peddlers of God's word, but as men of sincerity . . . in the sight of God we speak in Christ." The renouncing of disgraceful and underhanded ways has to do, evidently, not only with the framing of the message but with the character of the messengers: for if conscience be invoked in the hearers, its verdicts must be feared.

So, "we persuade men; but what we are is known to God, and I hope it is known also to your consciences . . . We put no obstacle in any one's way, so that no fault may be found with our ministry, but as servants of God we commend ourselves in every way: through great endurance, in afflictions, hardships, calamities, beatings, imprisonments, tumults, labours, watching, hunger; by purity, knowledge, forbearance, kindness, the Holy Spirit, genuine love, truthful speech, and the power of God; with the weapons of righteousness for the right hand and for the left; in honour and dishonour, in ill repute and good repute. We are treated as impostors, and yet are true; as unknown and yet well known; as dying, and behold we live; as punished and yet not killed;

as sorrowful, yet always rejoicing; as poor, yet making many rich; as having nothing and yet possessing everything."

In other words: by readiness to suffer for the truth proclaimed, by personal character in keeping with the truth proclaimed, by the use of weapons appropriate to the truth proclaimed, and by results confirming the truth proclaimed, we lay that truth, uncompromised, upon the consciences of those who hear and watch. This appeal from conscience to conscience, "commending the truth" by "commending ourselves", is the total presentation of the gospel: nothing short of this will do if the moral forces available within the listeners' souls are to be kindled to reinforce the impact of the evangel and awaken faith.

Nothing therefore can justify an aloof and impartial attitude on the part of the preacher, a "take it or leave it" approach to evangelism, that is content to have stated the truth and washes its hands of further responsibility. Truth spoken must be backed by truth lived, and loved, and passionately defended, incarnated, sacrificed for, if conscience, awakened, is to harass the hearer to conviction, repentance, and belief. The personal involvement of the preacher in the message and in the fate of the hearer is the cost of evangelistic power: but when the living word is so aimed by every force of conscientious speech and example at the quickened conscience of the listener — what divine energies are released, what miracles occur!

The Holy Spirit

Paul would phrase these affirmations in another way, and add greatly to their theological import, by ascribing all power in his ministry to the Holy Spirit. Sometimes indeed he speaks of the power of *Christ* resting upon him, of being able to do all things "in him who strengthens me". It is "Christ Jesus our Lord who has given me strength for this"; His is the "power at work within us"; His the power to be relied upon in the exercise of discipline (in the Corinthian Church); His the power "according to whose working" Paul was made a minister.

This is the tone which marks all Paul's references to the power manifest in his ministry. "The transcendent power belongs to God and not to us . . . The immeasurable greatness of his power in us who believe . . . who are strengthened with all power according to his glorious might . . . Our sufficiency is from God . . . It is God who establishes us with you in Christ . . . You are God's field, God's building."

The variation of phrase is not of first importance; the power of God, of Christ, is also "power of the Holy Spirit". Luke's story of the early Church is – from one point of view – a prolonged illustration of the superintendence, and endowment, and authority, and direction, and initiative, and restraint, and effectiveness of the Holy Spirit in the expanding experience of the Church: and while Luke shows remarkable independence of Paul's theology, there is no reason to suppose that they would not entirely agree on this interpretation of their common adventures. John, too, preserves the promise of Jesus that the witness of the disciples shall be empowered and carried to conviction by the testimony of the Spirit to Himself, as the Spirit of truth convincing the world and teaching the saints; and this likewise is consonant with Paul's thought.

Paul, indeed, might fairly be called the apostle of the Spirit. Much as we owe to him for clarifying the Church's conception of grace, for defining and defending justification by faith, for grasping and insisting that others grasp the universalist vision, it is not too much to say that his greatest contribution of all was to the Church's understanding of the Holy Spirit – and that not merely in doctrine but in experience. Just as no finer exposition of the Spirit's ministry in the life of the believer has ever been penned than Romans 8, so no more profound analysis of the "more excellent" signs of the Spirit's presence in the Church has ever been made than in the "first" letter to Corinth, with its very far-reaching moralisation of the doctrine, setting aside spectacles and wonders in favour of moral enrichment and Christlike love as the only sure proofs of the Spirit's endowment.

Yet Paul himself experienced the more theatrical manifestations of the Spirit, too. He recalls to the Corinthians that "the signs of a true apostle were performed among you in all patience, with signs and wonders and mighty works." Luke can say of the visit to Ephesus, "God did extraordinary miracles by the hands of Paul." Paul testifies, "I thank God that I speak in tongues more than you all" and tells of visions and revelations of the Lord and being "caught up to the third heaven". And he reminds the Thessalonians how "our gospel came to you not only in word, but as in power, and in the Holy Spirit, and with full conviction . . . You received the word in much affliction, with joy inspired by the Holy Spirit."

Of the evangelisation of Corinth Paul can say, deliberately contrasting various possible sources of popular power – wisdom, enticing speech, plausibility, signs – that though he was among them "in weakness and in much fear and trembling", his speech and his message were in demonstration of the Spirit and of power." And the implications of this are thoroughly worked out in forthright terms. The gospel is "a secret and hidden wisdom of God", and none can know the secrets of God but as God reveals them to us through the Spirit: "no one comprehends the thoughts of God except the Spirit of God." "And we impart this in words not taught by human wisdom but taught by the Spirit, interpreting spiritual truths to those who possess the Spirit."

That is a challenging statement of what is meant by a "Spirit-filled ministry". But so Paul looked upon his own work, and with humble gratitude could review its results: "In Christ Jesus I have reason to be proud of my work for God. For I will not venture to speak of anything except what Christ has wrought through me . . . by word and deed, by the power of signs and wonders, by the power of the Holy Spirit . . ."

To appreciate just how much it meant to Paul that the Spirit of God worked through his endeavours, spoke through his preaching, convinced men through his exposition of the truth, we must remember that to Paul's mind the whole pagan world was alive with superhuman powers and forces that worked their will upon human personality – demonic rulers, authorities, "principalities", the spirits at work in the disobedient, the rulers of this present darkness, spiritual hosts of wickedness in heavenly places against whom Christians must wrestle and pray. The "gods many and lords many" of paganism were, in Paul's eyes, agents of the devil, and a pagan altar was "the table of demons". Against so grim a background, only the certainty that another invasive Spirit, divine, holy, and infinitely more powerful, was on his side, and he himself the Spirit's agent, channel, and "vessel", could sustain his faith and labour. In his preaching, endurance, organisation, writing, and service, the Holy Spirit confronted the evil spirits and wrestled for the salvation of men. Unless that were true, all Christian effort was in vain.

The practical consequences of this confidence in the effectual power of the Holy Spirit as the operating force in all forms of Christian service are simple, but vital. One was that, as we have already noted, Paul insisted upon the necessity of prayer, an unceasing intercession on his behalf by colleagues and converts, if any lasting spiritual achievement was to be possible. It is right to lay emphasis upon efficiency and adequate training, upon experiment and thoroughness in devising methods of communication, propaganda, education and counselling: but if in fact the real work of God's kingdom must ever be in the last resort the work of the Holy Spirit alone, then prayerfulness is *the one vital efficiency* of the Christian worker. All else is well-meant waste of effort, unless by our constant waiting upon God the power of the Spirit is given through us an unlimited freedom, unhindered communication, and unhesitating response.

The other practical consequence of realising that the operating forces of Christian work derive from God's Spirit, concerns the attitude in which Christian work is approached. That dedicated, gifted, enthusiastic personality is the chosen agent of God is not questioned: but the inference from this is *not* that an aggressive, self-assertive manner betokens the "powerful" preacher, or teacher, or office-holder. The true consequence is that because the ultimate power is of God and not ours; because we, at our strongest, are only weak instruments for a force that is not under our control, the most we can do is to testify, declare, explain — and love — and then step aside that the Spirit Himself may wrestle with men. A certain self-effacement is absolutely necessary to a powerful ministry — if that power is to be the energy of the Holy Spirit and not simply the intense impression of a gifted personality. That strange apostolic humility, mingling diffidence with authority, which is part of the character of Paul, was at once the condition and the consequence of the Spirit's power in his life.

And that life was the most powerful the Church has ever known. We have approached its secrets: the daily renewal of the heart of the worker in the word and the presence of his Lord; the power within the word itself, plainly spoken and consistently lived out; the innate forces within human personality, released as the message assails the conscience; the ever-present energy of the Holy Spirit, the divine Ally of the gospel. Yet there is more to be experienced than can be expounded: and the heart must make its own experiments of the faithfulness of God, its own surrenders. But this is sure: never has the Church more desperately needed powerful men, or God more urgently sought the men He can trust with power.

What Shall We Then Say to This?

A CHRISTIAN PRIEST in Asia Minor about the middle of the second century offended his brethren, and was deposed from his ministry, because he had the bright but unusual idea of popularising Christian truths by means of religious romances – or at any rate by one, the story of Paul and a young, wealthy, ardent female convert from Iconium, named Thecla. In fact the story was anything but romantic, for it began with a broken engagement, proceeded through miraculous deliverance from martyrdom by fire, and ended somewhat tamely with sustained good works and a reputation for saintliness! What lends the whole enterprise a perennial interest is that the writer preserves a portrait of Paul which is so unflattering, so very unromantic, and so far in accord with the Corinthians' disparaging remarks about his bodily presence and "address", that one suspects some tenuous substratum of local memory behind the description:

"A man little of stature, thin-haired upon the head, crooked in the legs, of good state of body, with eyebrows joining, and a nose somewhat crooked; full of grace, for sometimes he appeared like a man, and sometimes had the face of an angel."

Such is a personal impression of Paul that lingered in one area of his missionary occupation. On the other hand, when we seek to summarise the total impression made by this figure upon history, the words that come most readily to mind are words like "towering", "prodigious", "colossal", "astonishing", "dynamic", "stupendous", and in this context that is not merely the language of publicists' hyperbole. Paradox is a dreadfully overworked category of modern Christian thought: yet paradox is simply inescapable. He *is* the towering figure of little stature, the enormously impressive unimpressive personality, the bearer of great treasure in an earthen vessel, the man whose tremendous strength lay in his besetting weakness, and who having nothing yet possessed all things.

He is Jew yet universalist; a child of his time and environment yet inexplicable apart from the transforming miracle of grace; impetuous and emotional yet profoundly analytical and argumentative; indomitable yet all too frequently deeply wounded; broadly sympathetic and adaptable yet inflexible; indebted yet independent; sure of his election yet nervous of failure, and certain of his divine commission yet fearful of judgement – indeed equally driven by fear and by love; equally aware of great privilege and of great responsibility; an individualist in faith yet supremely a team-man with a gift for friendship and valuing the Church corporate as few Christians have done; a man of the spiritual world and the timeless vision who teaches sound citizenship with a worldly realism and practicality; a complex personality charged with inherent spiritual forces of unusual energy and strength, and yet in the last resort but the channel of energies not his own and power only generated from on high.

All this has somehow to be reconciled – without being resolved away – in the one portrait of the apostle extraordinary, the ambassador who in truth could not be bound, the bondslave of Christ whose service he found perfect freedom.

For the deepest truth of all concerning Paul remains stubbornly paradoxical: that the same life could be so extortionately costly in toil and struggle, in opposition and adversity, in sheer physical pain, mental tension, and spiritual pressure, and yet be *at the same time* so charged with divine power, so profitable to others, so entirely, and richly, and variously, blessed of God. It seems we may need to revise very thoroughly all our modern estimates of what constitutes a life of "blessing", of guidance, of fruitfulness, and spiritual success.

For the sharp antithesis between the worker's personal experience and the work's cumulative effectiveness, which was forced on our attention by the different assessments of Paul's life reached by his contemporaries and his successors on the one hand and by Paul himself on the other, is wholly typical of Paul's experience. It is vividly illustrated – to offer only one summarising example – in the accounts we have of Paul's most outstandingly successful mission, that at Ephesus.

Luke, in a passage which aptly epitomises the whole Pauline saga, tells of extraordinary miracles done at the hands of Paul; of Judaism's promises and portents gloriously fulfilled under his ministry to certain disciples of John;

of two years of bold and sustained public argument; of the name of the Lord Jesus extolled throughout the city; of Paul's ministry insincerely "copied" — to their cost — by certain unbelievers; of such success that the idol-craftsmen's guild was moved to public protest; of the whole province of Asia evangelised and numerous daughter-Churches founded. Even when a confused and ineffectual mob threatened trouble, the city fathers and officials befriended Paul and ensured his safety. "So the word of the Lord grew and prevailed mightily."

Yet to piece together the Ephesian experience from Paul's own testimony is to realise the immense cost of that success. He lectures in the School of Tyrranus "from the fifth hour to the tenth" because these are the hours of the city's siesta: for the rest "these hands ministered to my necessities, and to those who were with me. In all things I have shown you that by so toiling one must help the weak . . ." He recalls to the Ephesian elders how he lived — "from the first day that I set foot in Asia, serving the Lord . . . with tears and with trials which befell me through the plots of the Jews . . . For three years I did not cease night or day to admonish you with tears."

In a letter written from Ephesus at this time he says: "To the present hour we hunger and thirst, we are ill-clad and buffeted and homeless, and we labour, working with our hands. When reviled, we bless; when persecuted, we endure; when slandered, we try to conciliate; we have become, *and are now,* as the refuse of the world, the offscouring of all things." That does not sound like the exaltation born of conscious success! In the same letter he adds: "Why am I in peril every hour? I protest, brethren, by my pride in you . . . I die every day! What do I gain if, humanly speaking, I fought with beasts at Ephesus? . . . I will stay in Ephesus until Pentecost, for a wide door for effective work has opened to me, and there are many adversaries."

Only a little later he is saying: "We do not want you to be ignorant, brethren, of the affliction we experienced in Asia; for we were so utterly, unbearably crushed that we despaired of life itself. Why, we felt that we had received the sentence of death; but . . . [God] delivered us from so deadly a peril, and he will deliver us . . ." The contrast between Luke's report of the Ephesus mission and Paul's confession of its cost could hardly be greater.

But that is characteristic of Paul's whole story. Paul's epitaphs are already written: one, by Luke, for his head — "So the word of the Lord grew and prevailed mightily"; the other, for his feet, written by Paul himself — "We were so utterly, unbearably crushed, but God delivered us."

For therein lies the final, provocative, ambiguous assessment. One can tell Paul's story as an exercise in Christian heroism, as a living illustration of limitless devotion, as the biography of one who loved Christ "till it hurt" and served Him faithfully until death. Or one can tell the story as a matchless example of divine power working its own will through human experience; as a frankly supernatural miracle-tale of a risen Lord and a divine Spirit "possessing" an individual, raising human effort to a cosmic significance and accomplishing "far more abundantly than all that we ask or think."

And for modern Christians, easy-going but power-hungry, the challenging, disturbing lesson is plain; while *both* accounts are true, *neither* is true without the other. The very last truth about Paul was already perceived by the first of his many biographers: "sometimes he appeared like a man, and sometimes had the face of an angel."